BISCUITS
AND
SCONES

BISCUITS

AND

SCONES

62 RECIPES
FROM BREAKFAST BISCUITS
TO HOMEY DESSERTS

By Elizabeth Alston

Illustrations by Sally Sturman

Clarkson N. Potter, Inc./Publishers

*Special thanks to
recipe development associates
Miriam Rubin and Claire Stancer,
to Milo O'Sullivan, Dionisia Colon,
Barbara Prisco and Paul Picciuto.*

. . . . . .

Text copyright © 1988 by Elizabeth Alston
Illustrations copyright © 1988 by Sally Sturman

Published by Clarkson N. Potter, Inc.
201 East 50th Street, New York, New York 10022.
Member of the Crown Publishing Group.
Random House, Inc. New York, Toronto, London, Sydney, Auckland
CLARKSON N. POTTER, POTTER, and colophon are
trademarks of Clarkson N. Potter, Inc.

Manufactured in the United States of America

Book design by Jan Melchior

Library of Congress Cataloging-in-Publication Data
Alston, Elizabeth
Biscuits and scones.
Includes index.
1. Biscuits.   2. Scones.   I. Title.
TX770.B55A44   1988   664'.7525   87-29110
ISBN 0-517-56345-2

16 15 14 13 12

CONTENTS

Introduction

vi
. . . . . .

Breakfast Favorites

14
. . . . . .

Lunch and Supper Specialties

34
. . . . . .

Homey Desserts

50
. . . . . .

Coffee and Teatime Treats

66
. . . . . .

Appetizers and Savory Snacks

88
. . . . . .

Index

104
. . . . . .

INTRODUCTION

Readers of my previous book, *Muffins*, will recollect the confusion I experienced when I found that in this country "muffins" describes individual baking powder breads baked in muffin cups, while I was familiar only with the yeast kind, known here as English muffins.

Biscuits and scones proved similarly perplexing. If you have visited England, you know that an English biscuit is an American cookie. As a newcomer to the States, I found biscuits closely related to what I knew as scones.

There are few recipes for scones in older American cookbooks. It is only recently, as scones have become a popular treat, that cookbooks and magazines have covered the subject at all.

The most straightforward definition of scones I came across was that scones contain eggs, while biscuits do not. To check out this theory, I consulted family cookbooks, since scones, like my family, are of Scottish origin and we ate them frequently. In my mother's handwritten cookbook (begun when she married my father), I found a whole range of scones, from the very simple to the rich.

The simplest scones were made only with white or whole-wheat flour, baking soda, and milk or buttermilk (real, from making butter). One such recipe was called "hairst," or harvest scones. Cut into huge, thick triangles and baked on a heavy iron griddle, these filling scones were carried to the harvesters in the fields, along with jars of runny rhubarb jam and huge enamel pots of black tea.

More elaborate recipes included fat, cane syrup or sugar, often currants or raisins, and yes, even an egg or two. These richer and smaller scones were made for family high tea, or afternoon tea, which was often a time when friends might drop by for a visit in pony and cart.

Based on admittedly limited research I am not going to attempt to define biscuits and scones. For the purposes of this book, most of the sweeter recipes are called scones, since that seems to coincide with the current American definition.

Perhaps scones became biscuits in the early days of the American South. Many Scots (including Alstons) emigrated to the South, especially around the Charleston area. There they met and perhaps even shared a cup of tea with French immigrants. Scones were popular fare, if this quote from the first edition of *Charleston Receipts*, published in 1950, is any indication. "Among the rich and crumbly delights to serve with jams and marmalades, are Scones, those our Grandmothers loved to make; not too sweet, not too hearty, but just right as a morsel of goodness to go with the hospitable gesture of a cup of tea and a good gossip."

Biscuit is a French word (pronounced biss-kwee) with a variety of meanings and is applied to many kinds of biscuits, according to *Larousse Gastronomique*, including *biscuits de guerre* (army rations of flour and water) and *biscuits de patisserie* (sweet biscuits). My guess is that French cooks dubbed the plainer type of Scottish scone "*biscuit de* something" and that eventually the "*de* something" was dropped.

Biscuits and scones require few ingredients, a minimum of tools, and no special baking pans. In addition, they are incredibly easy to make. Biscuits and scones are wonderful to eat with other foods, but the doughs can also be used for many kinds of delicious dishes, from old-fashioned desserts such as slumps and pandowdies, to newer appetizer pies. I've included both.

In "Breakfast Favorites," you'll find plain biscuits, many made from whole-grain flours, that are perfect accompaniments to eggs and bacon, marmalade, and preserves. (They make excellent dinner breads, too, with fried chicken, rich stews, or hearty salads.) You'll also find directions for savory Scottish scones made with potatoes and green onions and recipes for not-too-sweet scones, stuffed with raisins, cranberries, and prunes, that make delightful additions to the breakfast breadbasket. For festive occasions you'll find a quick version of cinnamon-pecan rolls (also known as sticky buns) and that Easter favorite, hot cross buns.

Look in "Lunch and Supper Specialties" for soup with corn biscuit dumplings, for a lamb potpie with a red wine gravy that makes a truly special company meal, and for a Canadian pork pie that has a quick biscuit crust instead of the more usual pie crust.

In "Homey Desserts" you'll find a recipe for a true, all-American strawberry shortcake, along with a divine caramel-banana shortcake and a collection of updated Early American favorites such as pandowdy and cobbler.

"Coffee and Teatime Treats" offers biscuit and scone recipes that are excellent instead of coffee cake for breakfast or with midmorning or midafternoon coffee or tea. Try chocolate-chip scones with a steaming cup of French roast coffee; orange-almond and apricot swirl scones are particularly good with mandarin orange spice tea.

In "Appetizers and Savory Snacks" you'll find ideas for finger foods for your next party, as well as more substantial fare such as a fresh mushroom appetizer pie (which I also love to serve for supper) and a tomato—sour cream tart. These are perfect to serve when you invite friends for a drink and want to make one special thing, when you need something fairly substantial before going to a movie or a ball game, or as a light lunch with a glass of wine.

I think you will get an enormous amount of pleasure out of even a small repertoire of biscuits and scones. But before you reach for the flour or turn on the oven, please read the following basic information. It will help make you a more confident baker.

INGREDIENTS

FLOUR

For flaky, light, traditional biscuits, use bleached or unbleached white flour.

Use whole-grain flours such as barley, rye, or oat, alone or mixed with all-purpose flour, for extra flavor and better nutrition. These flours produce a much crumblier textured biscuit than wheat flour. Whole-wheat flour tends to make rather dry scones and biscuits, so be careful not to overbake them.

FAT

Fat makes biscuits and scones tender and flaky. Use butter or margarine or one of the butter-margarine blends. Use *plain*, preferably unsalted, butter, not whipped, diet, or soft butter.

Many excellent bakers feel that lard or solid vegetable shortening produces the lightest biscuits. You can substitute either of those fats for butter or margarine or use a combination.

Olive oil is used in several recipes. It imparts a lovely flavor and is very easy to use. Instead of being rubbed into the flour (as butter is), it is stirred in with the liquid ingredients.

LEAVENING

Most of the biscuits and scones in this book are raised, or leavened, with double-acting baking powder, which contains one raising agent that starts creating bubbles (causing the dough to rise) when liquid is added. The second agent is activated by oven heat. (Once the can is opened, baking powder gradually loses its effectiveness, so mark the date on the can and replace it after a year.)

A few of the recipes include baking soda. Mixed with buttermilk, baking soda works as a leavening and also neutralizes the acidity of the buttermilk. Or it may be used to neutralize other acid ingredients, such as brown sugar, molasses, or apricots.

Cream of tartar is occasionally combined with baking soda for an old-fashioned but very effective leavening.

Self-rising flour, flour with the baking powder and salt already mixed in, was once commonly available. Now it is found mainly in the South. It speeds biscuit making because it eliminates some measuring. You may substitute self-rising flour in recipes calling for all-purpose flour, salt, and baking powder.

LIQUID

For tender, moist biscuits and scones use milk, buttermilk, or plain yogurt, but do not make changes without first studying the recipe. If you want to use buttermilk or plain yogurt when the recipe calls for milk, add ½ teaspoon of baking soda to the flour for each cup of buttermilk.

If you have only regular milk in the house but need buttermilk, pour 1 tablespoon of lemon juice, or a simple vinegar such as rice, cider, or distilled white, into a glass measuring cup. Fill to the 1-cup mark with milk. Stir, let the mixture stand a minute or two, then proceed with the recipe. (For ⅔ or ¾ cup milk use 2 teaspoons of lemon juice or vinegar.)

Buttermilk powder, which works so well for most recipes, tends to impart a sweetish flavor to biscuits and scones. If you use it, follow package directions.

For extra-rich biscuits and scones you may use half-and-half or heavy cream instead of milk.

MAKING PERFECT BISCUITS AND SCONES

OVEN

Modern ovens heat to the proper temperature in 10 minutes or so, about the time it takes to make a biscuit or scone dough. So the first step is to check that one oven rack is in the middle (unless the recipe specifies otherwise) and turn the oven on. I always keep a thermometer in my oven to check the accuracy of the thermostat.

COOKIE SHEET

Just about any metal cookie sheet, baking pan, or even a pizza pan will work fine, and whether it has a dark or very bright, shiny finish makes very little difference. In tests, I found that the least successful cookie sheet for biscuits and scones was the cushion type. Cookie sheets with a nonstick finish are excellent and need only a wipe with a damp cloth after use.

MEASURING

For best results, measure ingredients correctly. Use glass measuring cups for liquids (bend over and check at eye level), metal or plastic cups for dry ingredients and solids such as shortening or raisins.

To measure flour, use the following stir, spoon, and sweep method:

Using a metal spoon, give the flour a quick stir in bag or canister.

Spoon the flour loosely into an exact-size cup measure until overflowing; do not press the flour down or tap cup on table.

Draw the back of a knife across top of the cup, sweeping away excess flour. Tip the measured flour into a bowl.

Using exact-size cups means using, for example, a ½ cup plus a ¼ cup measure to measure ¾ cup flour. Do not try to measure ¾ cup flour in a 1-cup measure.

Since granulated sugar is much heavier than flour, you can scoop it from the bag or canister with the measuring cup and sweep off the excess with the back of a knife.

Moist brown sugar is measured differently: pack it firmly into a metal or plastic cup measure until it is level with the top.

For baking powder and spices, use standard measuring spoons of good quality (for accuracy). Dip the spoon in the container, fill to overflowing, then sweep off excess with the back of a knife. Or pour the spice into a spoon over a small piece of wax paper, which you can then use to pour the excess back into the jar.

For easy measuring, I've called for tablespoons of butter wherever possible. If wrappers are not marked, keep in mind: *4 ounces butter or margarine equals 8 tablespoons, or ½ cup.* (One stick or cube of butter weighs 4 ounces.)

Use metal or plastic cup measures for solid vegetable shortening. Pack the shortening into the correct-size measure with a rubber or metal spatula; level the surface. Scrape the shortening right into the flour; do not try to cut it into pieces as you do with butter or margarine.

RUBBING IN THE BUTTER

Put the dry ingredients (flour, baking powder) into a large bowl—one about 10 inches in diameter is comfortable to work in. Mix these ingredients very thoroughly with a wooden spoon or with one hand.

Cut the butter into small chunks and drop them into the flour. To rub the fat into the flour, start with a pastry blender (four rigid wire loops on a handle) and quickly chop the fat and flour, turning the bowl slowly with your other hand. If you don't have a pastry blender, hold a table knife in each hand and chop away. Or press the lumps of fat between thumb and fingers. You can also use a food processor (see page 10).

Chopping cuts the fat into smaller and smaller pieces. When the pieces are about the size of peas, switch to fingertips. Put your hands in the bowl with the backs of your fingers almost touching the bottom and fingertips almost touching. Pick up some of the flour mixture in each hand and rub your thumbs across your fingers from little finger to index finger, through the flour mixture. Repeat this motion over and over, working quickly and flipping the mixture around, until it looks like fine, slightly damp granules. At this point the fat has been rubbed into the flour properly.

Now add sugar, currants, or nuts if called for in the recipe. Toss the mixture with your fingers to distribute the added ingredients evenly.

You may stop at this point, cover the bowl tightly with plastic wrap, and refrigerate. Later—even a few days later—you can add the liquid and continue the recipe.

ADDING THE LIQUID

A sturdy fork, larger than a dinner fork, is ideal for mixing the liquid into the flour mixture. (My fork has a comfortable wooden handle.)

Pour the liquid over the flour mixture and start stirring with the fork. The particles of fat and flour will soon start clumping together to form a dough, which may be quite soft or very stiff, depending on the recipe. With practice you will soon learn to tell if the dough feels right. If there really doesn't seem to be enough liquid to moisten all the particles, add a little more milk or water, not more than 1 tablespoon at a time.

If the dough seems unworkably soft, you can let it stand for a couple of minutes while the flour absorbs some of the liquid. If that doesn't do the trick, flour the board generously before kneading. But don't overdo it; keep the dough as soft as you can or the results will be dry.

Depending on the individual recipe and the amount of liquid called for, the dough may end up as one clump in your bowl, or in a lot of bits and pieces that you gather together with one hand and press into a ball.

FOOD PROCESSOR

A food processor fitted with the steel blade will rub or cut fat into flour in a snap. Put the dry ingredients in the work bowl and process a second or two to mix. Scatter cut-up butter over the flour. Process, using the on-off motion, until the mixture looks like fine granules.

If the recipe calls for the addition of ingredients such as raisins or chocolate chips, tip the mixture into a mixing bowl and complete the recipe by hand.

If only liquid is to be added, pour it all over the surface of the flour. Using the on-off motion, process just until the dough forms a clump. Dough made in a food processor does not require kneading.

KNEADING

Yeast doughs are kneaded to develop an elastic quality. Biscuit doughs are kneaded briefly and only to complete the mixing.

Sprinkle a countertop or board lightly with flour. Put the dough on the floured surface and lightly flour your fingers. To knead, lift the edge of the dough farthest away from you, bring it toward you, and press it down lightly into the center of the ball of dough. Turn the dough slightly as you press. Repeat the motion rhythmically; each gather and press is a "knead." The dough is kneaded enough when it feels silky and looks fairly smooth.

When kneading is completed, the dough will be more or less in a ball, smooth on the underside, all folds and gathers on the top. Turn the dough over, smooth side up. Clean off the work surface and sprinkle lightly with flour so the dough doesn't stick while you are shaping it.

SHAPING BISCUITS AND SCONES

Very soft mixtures, such as for drop scones, are neither kneaded nor rolled. The batter is simply spooned or measured onto a cookie sheet.

For triangular biscuits and scones that require no cutters and usually no rolling pin, cut the kneaded dough in half. Briefly knead each half into a ball, turn over so the smooth side is up, pat into a circle, and cut into wedges with a sharp knife. This is an easy and fuss-free shaping method.

For traditional round biscuits and scones, put the kneaded dough, smooth side up, on a lightly floured work surface. Sprinkle a little flour on a rolling pin and rub it over the pin with your hand.

Roll the pin lightly back and forth across the top of the dough, exerting only light pressure. Do not roll over the edges. Every two or three rollings, lift the dough slightly and turn it about one third around to make sure it is not sticking to the surface.

Roll the dough to desired thickness (biscuit dough rises about half as much again when baked). Dip a plain, round biscuit cutter into flour and cut straight down through the dough without twisting the cutter. Cut the circles as close together as practical. Put the cut biscuits on a cookie sheet. Gather the scraps of dough together (don't reknead) and pat to desired thickness. Cut out more biscuits. Twist the remaining scraps together and place on the cookie sheet.

For soft-sided biscuits, arrange uncooked biscuits close together on the cookie sheet. For crusty sides, leave at least a 1-inch space between biscuits and scones.

BAKING

Bake only one sheet of biscuits or scones at a time, and place cookie sheet on the oven rack so that the sides do not touch the oven walls or door. You need space all around the cookie sheet to allow hot air to circulate evenly.

Ovens vary in baking quality, even if their thermostats are on target. When you put a batch of biscuits or scones in the oven, set the timer for just under the shortest length of time recommended in the recipe.

HOW TO TELL WHEN BISCUITS AND SCONES ARE DONE

When you check for doneness, put three senses on the alert: smell, sight, and touch.

When biscuits and scones are cooked, they *smell* done. They no longer *look* raw; they are of good color. Finished color varies according to the recipe, and I've tried to indicate what shade to look for. When you *touch* biscuits that are cooked, they feel springy but firm, indicating that there is no uncooked dough still in the center. Scones and biscuits continue to cook after they have been taken from the oven, but overbaked scones and biscuits can be dry.

It will take the inexperienced baker only one or two batches to feel confident about judging doneness.

COOLING BISCUITS AND SCONES

I thought Mother wrapped cooling scones in a linen towel to hide them from hungry eyes. Actually, the loose wrapping slows down the cooling process and keeps the biscuits and scones from getting soggy or drying out. Arrange a cotton or linen dish towel so that half covers a wire cooling rack and half lies on the counter. Put the scones in a single layer on the cloth-covered rack and fold the rest of the towel loosely over them.

Serving biscuits and scones fresh from the oven may sound romantic, but most need at least 30 minutes' cooling time to develop full flavor.

FREEZING BISCUITS AND SCONES

Cool baked biscuits and scones completely. Wrap tightly in heavy plastic bags, pressing out as much air as possible.

To reheat, spread frozen scones or biscuits on a cookie sheet and heat about 5 minutes in a 250° F. oven.

Most biscuits and scones can also be frozen before baking. After cutting or shaping, freeze them on a cookie sheet or tray lined with wax paper. When hard, wrap tightly in heavy plastic bags and store in the freezer. Bake frozen, a minute or two longer than specified in the recipe.

BREAKFAST FAVORITES

VERMONT MAPLE–CORN
DROP BISCUITS

Almost any regular rolled-out biscuits can be converted into drop biscuits by adding enough extra liquid so the dough is soft enough to be dropped on the cookie sheet. These are excellent with bacon or ham.

1 cup coarse-ground yellow cornmeal

1 cup all-purpose flour

1 tablespoon baking powder

¼ teaspoon salt

¼ cup maple or maple-flavor syrup

Milk

5 tablespoons cold unsalted butter, cut up

Heat oven to 425° F. Put cornmeal, flour, baking powder, and salt into a large bowl. Stir to mix well.

Measure maple syrup in a glass cup measure. Add milk to the ⅔ cup mark.

Add butter to the flour mixture and cut in with a pastry blender or rub in with your fingers, until mixture looks like fine granules.

Add the milk mixture and stir with a fork until a very soft dough forms.

Drop ¼ cupfuls of dough 2 inches apart onto an ungreased cookie sheet.

Bake 12 to 14 minutes, until pale golden brown. Cool, loosely covered with a dish towel, on a wire rack.

GOOD-WITH-ANYTHING
BAKING POWDER BISCUITS

....

10 TO 12 2½-INCH BISCUITS
OR 12 TRIANGULAR BISCUITS

Here they are, the simplest, plainest biscuits of all, the longtime favorite bread of the South. Serve these biscuits as a breakfast bread with eggs and bacon, sausage, or a country-ham steak. Enjoy them, too, as a dinner bread. For a true North Carolina dinner, pile warm biscuits in a basket and serve them with honey and butter, crisp fried chicken, and at least two vegetables.

> *2 cups all-purpose flour*
>
> *1 tablespoon baking powder*
>
> *½ teaspoon salt*
>
> *5 tablespoons cold unsalted butter or margarine, cut up, or ⅓ cup solid vegetable shortening (see note)*
>
> *⅔ cup milk*

Heat oven to 450° F. Put flour, baking powder, and salt into a large bowl; stir to mix well.

Add butter and cut in with a pastry blender or rub in with your fingers, until the mixture looks like fine granules.

Add milk and stir with a fork until a soft dough forms. Turn out dough onto a lightly floured board and give 10 to 15 kneads. For classic round biscuits, roll dough to an 8- to 8½-inch circle (½ to ¾ inch thick). Cut out with a 2- or

2½-inch plain biscuit cutter; press the scraps together, roll out, and cut. Place biscuits on an ungreased cookie sheet, sides touching for soft sides, apart for crisper ones. For triangular, no-cutter-needed biscuits, cut dough in half. Knead each half lightly into a ball, turn smooth side up, and pat or roll into a 6-inch circle. Cut each circle into 6 wedges. Place on cookie sheet as for round biscuits.

Bake 12 to 14 minutes, until medium golden brown. Line a wire cooling rack with a linen or cotton dish towel. Put the hot biscuits on the cloth and fold the cloth loosely over them. Cool at least 30 minutes for best flavor.

NOTE: Scrape shortening straight from the measuring cup into the flour without trying to cut it up.

....
VARIATIONS

Buttermilk Biscuits. Use buttermilk or plain yogurt instead of sweet milk. Reduce baking powder to 2 teaspoons and add ¼ teaspoon baking soda to the flour.

Oat Biscuits. Replace 1 cup of the all-purpose flour with 1 cup old-fashioned oats ground to a powder in a blender or food processor. (If you use quick-cooking oats, reduce salt to ¼ teaspoon.) Cool the biscuits at least 15 minutes but preferably a couple of hours, to allow the flavor to develop. Delicious with Gouda or Saga blue cheese, or with marmalade for breakfast.

Rye, Barley, or Cornmeal Biscuits. Replace 1 cup of the all-purpose flour with 1 cup rye flour, barley flour, or coarse-ground cornmeal. For cornmeal-chive biscuits, add ¼ cup snipped fresh chives to flour mixture just before adding milk.

CHARLOTTE WALKER'S BREAKFAST BERRY SHORTCAKES

Food consultant Charlotte Walker serves these for brunch in her San Francisco home. Start the Crème Fraîche the day before so it has time to thicken and chill. The shortcake biscuits are very rich and crumbly, and like most biscuits or shortcakes, they may be frozen unbaked.

> **3 cups all-purpose flour**
>
> **¼ cup granulated sugar**
>
> **2 tablespoons baking powder**
>
> **¾ teaspoon salt**
>
> **½ pound (2 sticks) cold unsalted butter, cut up**
>
> **⅔ cup milk**
>
> **2 quarts mixed berries: strawberries, blueberries, raspberries, blackberries, or olallieberries**
>
> **Additional sugar for sprinkling**
>
> **1 egg beaten with 1 tablespoon water**
>
> **Crème Fraîche (recipe follows)**

Put flour, ¼ cup sugar, baking powder, and salt into a large bowl; stir to mix well.

Add butter and cut in with a pastry blender or rub in with your fingers until the mixture looks like fine granules. Add milk; stir with a fork to form a soft dough, adding more milk if needed.

Turn out dough onto a floured surface and give 8 to 10 kneads. Roll or pat dough to a ¾-inch thickness. Cut out shortcakes with a 2- or 2½-inch round cutter; reroll and cut the scraps. Place apart on an ungreased cookie sheet. Cover with plastic wrap and refrigerate 30 minutes or up to 24 hours.

Hull the strawberries, then slice them into a bowl (or leave whole if tiny); sprinkle with a little sugar. Add other berries; toss gently.

Heat oven to 375° F. Brush shortcakes with beaten egg. Bake 14 to 16 minutes, or until lightly browned. Serve the shortcakes warm in a basket. Let everyone split a warm shortcake and fill with berries and Crème Fraîche.

CRÈME FRAÎCHE

Mix 2 cups heavy cream (not ultrapasteurized) and 2 tablespoons freshly squeezed lemon juice in a jar. Cover and let stand 8 to 12 hours at room temperature. Refrigerate; the mixture will become very thick. Serve as is, or, if fruit is tart, stir in about 2 tablespoons mild honey. Makes 2 cups.

CARDAMOM-PRUNE DROP SCONES

A delicate scone filled with chunks of moist prunes. Prunes cut easily with an oiled knife or kitchen shears.

   2 cups all-purpose flour

   2 teaspoons baking powder

   1/2 teaspoon baking soda

   3/4 teaspoon ground cardamom seeds

   1/4 teaspoon salt

   3/4 cup sour cream

   1 large egg

   1/4 cup granulated sugar

   1 teaspoon freshly grated lemon peel

   8 tablespoons (1 stick) cold unsalted butter, cut up

   3/4 cup (4 1/2 ounces) finely cut moist prunes

Heat oven to 375° F. Put flour, baking powder, baking soda, cardamom, and salt into a large bowl; mix well.

In another bowl, beat sour cream, egg, sugar, and lemon peel until well blended.

Add butter to the flour mixture and cut in with a pastry blender or rub in with your fingers, until the mixture looks like fine granules. Add prunes and toss to distribute evenly.

Add sour cream mixture and stir with a spoon until a sticky dough forms.

Drop ⅓ cupfuls of dough 2 inches apart on an ungreased cookie sheet.

Bake 20 to 25 minutes, until golden brown. Cool, loosely covered with a dish towel, on a wire rack.

QUICK CINNAMON-PECAN ROLLS

16 ROLLS

Called "quick" because the crust is a biscuit, not a time-consuming yeast dough. These fragrant rolls are not too sticky or sweet. If you love the truly gooey kind, double the caramel topping.

CRUST

1 **cup all-purpose flour**

1½ **teaspoons baking powder**

⅛ **teaspoon salt**

3 **tablespoons cold unsalted butter, cut up**

⅓ **cup milk**

CARAMEL TOPPING

¼ **cup plus ¼ cup light or dark brown sugar, firmly packed**

½ **cup shelled pecans, coarsely chopped**

2 **tablespoons milk**

½ **teaspoon ground cinnamon**

1½ **tablespoons very soft or melted butter**

To make the crust, put flour, baking powder, and salt into a large bowl; stir to mix well. Add butter and cut in with a pastry blender or rub in with your fingers, until mixture looks like fine granules.

Add milk and stir with a fork until a soft dough forms. Turn out dough onto a lightly floured surface and give 10 to

12 kneads. Pat into a rectangle; wrap and refrigerate while you prepare topping.

Heat oven to 425° F. To make topping, put ¼ cup of the brown sugar, ¼ cup of the pecans, milk, and cinnamon in the bottom of an 8- or 9-inch round layer cake pan. Stir to mix well; spread evenly.

On a lightly floured board, roll dough into a rectangle about 16 × 12 inches, with a long side near you. Brush dough with soft butter, except for a 1-inch border along the farthest edge. Mix the remaining ¼ cup brown sugar with the remaining ¼ cup nuts; sprinkle over the butter.

Roll up the dough jelly-roll fashion, starting from the long edge nearest you. Cut the roll into 16 slices. Arrange the slices, cut side up and slightly apart, on top of the brown sugar mixture in the pan.

Bake 25 minutes, or until nicely browned. Invert immediately onto a serving plate and remove pan. Let cool 20 minutes before serving.

RAISIN SCONES

12 SCONES

  2 **cups all-purpose flour**
  2 **teaspoons baking powder**
 ½ **teaspoon baking soda**
 ½ **teaspoon ground nutmeg**
 ½ **teaspoon salt**
  8 **tablespoons (1 stick) cold unsalted butter, cut up**
  1 **cup raisins**
  2 **tablespoons granulated sugar**
    Yolk of 1 large egg
 ¾ **cup buttermilk or plain yogurt**
    White of 1 large egg
    Additional sugar for sprinkling

Heat oven to 375° F. Put flour, baking powder, baking soda, nutmeg, and salt into a large bowl; stir to mix well. Add butter and cut in with a pastry blender or rub in with your fingers, until the mixture looks like fine granules. Add raisins and sugar; toss to distribute evenly.

Add egg yolk to buttermilk in a measuring cup and whisk with a fork to blend. Pour over the flour mixture and stir with a fork until a soft dough forms.

Turn out dough onto a lightly floured surface and give 10 to 12 kneads. Cut dough in half. Knead each half briefly into a ball; turn smooth side up and pat into a 6-inch circle. Cut into 6 wedges, but do not separate wedges.

In a small bowl, beat the egg white with a fork until just broken up. Brush the top of each scone with egg white and sprinkle lightly with sugar. With a pancake turner, carefully transfer the two cut circles to an ungreased cookie sheet. If necessary, reshape circles so that the 6 wedges in each are touching. (This will keep the raisins from burning.)

Bake 18 to 22 minutes, until medium brown. Cool on a wire rack; after 5 minutes pull the wedges apart and cover loosely with a dish towel.

NOTE: Egg white and sugar can be added before freezing the unbaked scones.

....
VARIATION

Coarse Whole-Wheat—Raisin Scones. Replace 1 cup all-purpose flour with 1 cup whole-wheat flour, and add ½ cup miller's bran to the flour mixture. Omit nutmeg.

MOTHER BATHIA'S SCOTTISH TATTIE SCONES

16 TRIANGLES

I like to add scallions to Mother's plain scones, which she baked on the heavy iron griddle she brought from Aberdeenshire when she came to England as a bride. "Tattie" is potato with a Scottish accent. These scones are super for breakfast with thick-sliced bacon and scrambled eggs. They rise very little and reheat well.

1/2 pound (1 large) russet baking potato
4 tablespoons (1/2 stick) unsalted butter
1/4 cup sliced green onions (scallions)
1 large egg
1/2 teaspoon salt
1/4 teaspoon freshly ground black pepper
3/4 cup all-purpose flour
Additional flour as needed

Peel the potato and cut into 1-inch slices. Put in a small saucepan with cold water to cover. Cover the pan and simmer over medium heat until potato is very tender when pierced with a knife. Pour off all the water. Put the pan over low heat for about 1 minute to dry the potato. Mash potato with a fork—small lumps are okay. Measure 1 cupful and put into a medium-size bowl.

While the potato cooks, melt butter with green onions in a small saucepan over moderately low heat. Add to the mashed potato along with egg, salt, and pepper. Beat with a spoon to mix well. Lightly stir in ½ cup of the flour, then as much of the remaining ¼ cup flour as needed to make a stiff dough.

Turn out dough onto a lightly floured board and give 20 kneads to mix well. Cut dough in half. Roll or pat one half into a 7-inch circle. Cut into 8 wedges.

Heat an electric skillet to 325° F. or heat a heavy iron or nonstick griddle or skillet over medium-low heat. Sprinkle about 2 tablespoons of flour over the bottom of the skillet (use a dredger if you have one). Arrange scones—sides not touching—in the skillet. Let cook, uncovered, 5 to 7 minutes, or until scones start to puff slightly and turn golden brown on the underside. (Adjust heat as necessary so scones don't scorch.) Turn scones and cook 3 to 5 minutes longer, until lightly browned. Repeat with remaining dough. Cool, loosely covered with a dish towel, on a wire rack for about 10 minutes before serving.

BIG BARLEY-CURRANT SCONE

1 ROUND LOAF

Barley flour makes this scone soft and crumbly. It is absolutely delicious sliced and served with butter for breakfast or with cheese for a light lunch.

1 cup milk

2 tablespoons granulated sugar

½ cup Zante currants (see note)

1½ cups barley flour

1 cup all-purpose flour

1 tablespoon baking powder

½ teaspoon salt

4 tablespoons (½ stick) cold unsalted butter, cut up

½ cup coarsely chopped walnuts

Check that one rack is in bottom third of the oven and heat oven to 425° F.

Measure milk in a 2-cup glass measure; stir in sugar, then currants.

Put flours, baking powder, and salt into a large bowl; stir to mix well. Add butter and cut in with a pastry blender or rub in with your fingers, until the mixture looks like fine granules. Stir in walnuts.

Stir the milk mixture, add to the bowl of flour, and mix with a fork until a soft dough forms.

Turn out dough onto a lightly floured surface and give 10 to 12 kneads. Put the dough smooth side up on an ungreased cookie sheet and pat into an 8-inch circle. Cut the top into a diamond pattern by pressing the edge of a ruler or the blunt edge of a chef's knife ¼ to ½ inch deep into the dough and making 5 lines in each direction.

Bake 20 minutes; turn heat down to 350° F. and bake 7 to 10 minutes longer, or until the loaf is golden brown and acquires a done look. Cool on a wire rack at least 1 hour before slicing.

NOTE: Zante currants, like raisins, are dried grapes. Store in a tightly closed container so they don't get hard or too dry. To soften, soak 10 minutes in very hot water. Drain well before adding to milk.

HOT CROSS SCONES

The traditional Good Friday treat, made quickly with baking powder instead of yeast. The flavor is true, but the texture is, of course, completely different.

2½ cups all-purpose flour

1 tablespoon baking powder

1 teaspoon ground cinnamon (see note)

¼ teaspoon ground allspice

¼ teaspoon ground cloves

½ teaspoon salt

8 tablespoons (1 stick) cold unsalted butter, cut up

½ cup Zante currants or dark raisins

¼ cup granulated sugar

2 tablespoons finely chopped candied orange, lemon, or grapefruit peel (optional)

⅔ cup milk

ICING

⅓ cup confectioners' sugar

1¼ to 1½ teaspoons milk

Heat oven to 375° F. Put flour, baking powder, spices, and salt into a large bowl; stir to mix well. Add butter and cut in with a pastry blender or rub in with your fingers, until the mixture looks like fine granules.

Add currants, sugar and peel; toss to distribute evenly. Add milk and stir with a fork until a soft dough forms.

Turn out dough onto a lightly floured board and give 10 to 12 kneads. Form into a ball; cut into 8 wedges. Form each wedge into a ball and put apart on an ungreased cookie sheet. Bake 10 to 15 minutes, or until medium brown. Cool 5 minutes, loosely covered with a cloth, on a wire rack.

Mix confectioners' sugar and milk in a cup or small bowl to make a smooth, thick icing. Using the tip of a teaspoon, make a cross of icing on top of each scone. Let cool, uncovered, 5 minutes more, then cover again with the cloth. May be served right away.

NOTE: You may use 1½ teaspoons pumpkin pie spice instead of the spices listed.

CRANBERRY SCONES

....

8 LARGE SCONES

If the cranberries are very large, snip or cut each one in half—not nearly so arduous a task as it sounds. Freeze plenty of berries in season so you can enjoy these year-round.

2/3 cup buttermilk or plain yogurt

1 large egg

3 cups all-purpose flour

4 teaspoons baking powder

1/2 teaspoon baking soda

1/2 teaspoon salt

8 tablespoons (1 stick) cold unsalted butter, cut up

1 cup fresh or frozen cranberries

1/2 cup granulated sugar

1 teaspoon freshly grated orange peel (optional)

1 tablespoon butter, at room temperature

Heat oven to 375° F. Measure buttermilk in a 2-cup glass measure; beat in egg with a fork.

Put flour, baking powder, baking soda, and salt into a large bowl. Stir to mix well. Add the 8 tablespoons butter and cut in with a pastry blender or rub in with your fingers, until the mixture looks like fine granules.

Add cranberries, sugar, and orange peel; toss lightly to distribute evenly. Add buttermilk mixture. Stir with a fork until a soft dough forms.

Turn out dough onto a lightly floured board and give 5 to 6 kneads, just until well mixed. Form dough into a ball; cut into 8 wedges. Form each wedge into a ball and place on an ungreased cookie sheet.

Bake 20 to 25 minutes, or until medium brown. Remove to a wire rack. Brush with the 1 tablespoon of soft butter. Let cool, uncovered, at least 1 hour before serving.

LUNCH AND SUPPER SPECIALTIES

HAM OR SMOKED
TURKEY BISCUITS

....

10 TO 25 BISCUITS (DEPENDING ON SIZE)

O n buffet tables in the South there is almost always a big country ham, a roast or smoked turkey, and piles of baking powder biscuits. For a small party, you can buy meats already sliced (keep them covered so they don't dry out). You can fill the biscuits in the kitchen—or put out the fixings and let guests fill their own. If you like, spread with plain or mustard butter before filling. At holiday time put out cranberry sauce or a fruit chutney such as orange or mango. The biscuits can range in size from 1½ to 2½ inches.

> **Dough for Good-with-Anything Baking Powder Biscuits (page 16)**
>
> ½ **pound thinly sliced smoked turkey or fully cooked ham, preferably a dry country ham from Virginia, Tennessee, or New York State**

Heat oven to 450° F. Roll out dough to a ½-inch thickness. Cut out with plain round biscuit cutter (see note). Bake 12 to 15 minutes, until lightly browned. Cool, loosely wrapped in a dish towel, on a wire rack.

Pull biscuits apart, fill with turkey or ham, and eat out of hand.

N O T E : A 2½-inch cutter will yield 10 to 12 biscuits; a 2-inch cutter about 16 biscuits; a 1½-inch cutter about 25.

BISCUIT PISSALADIÈRE

A close relative of pizza, this onion-and-tomato-topped bread was originally a specialty of Nice. Here, a quick, soft biscuit crust replaces the traditional yeast crust. Best eaten within an hour or two of baking.

TOPPING

- **4 tablespoons olive oil**
- **4 cups chopped onions (from 1 to 1½ pounds yellow, red, or white onions, or a mixture)**
- **1 can (2 ounces) flat anchovy fillets, drained**
- **¾ teaspoon dried rosemary or thyme leaves**
- **¼ teaspoon salt**
- **1 can (14½ ounces) peeled tomatoes, drained**
- **8 to 10 black olives (California ripe, oil-cured, or Greek Kalamata**

BISCUIT CRUST

- **2 cups all-purpose flour**
- **1 tablespoon baking powder**
- **1 teaspoon salt**
- **½ cup olive oil**
- **½ cup milk or chicken broth**
  Sprigs of fresh thyme or rosemary for decoration

To make topping, heat 3 tablespoons of the oil in a heavy, medium-size saucepan or large skillet over medium heat. Stir in onions, 2 anchovy fillets, ½ teaspoon of the herb, and the salt. Cover and cook about 30 minutes, adjusting the heat if the mixture is cooking too fast and stirring every 5 minutes or so, until onions are translucent, very tender, and golden, but not really brown. (The onions will cook down considerably.)

While the onions cook, make the crust. Mix flour, baking powder, and salt in a large bowl. Add olive oil and milk. Stir with a wooden spoon until a soft, pasty dough forms.

Put dough on a large, ungreased cookie sheet. Roll into a rectangle about 15 × 12 inches. Put in the freezer until ready to add the topping.

Chop tomatoes and put in a strainer to complete draining. Cut each remaining anchovy fillet into 2 or 3 lengthwise strips. Pit olives and slice, or cut into thin strips.

At this point, if desired, everything can be put on hold: the crust covered and returned to the freezer; the various filling components covered and refrigerated for up to three days.

Heat oven to 425° F. Spread tomatoes over the crust, then onions. Decorate with anchovies and sprinkle with olives, the remaining ¼ teaspoon of herb, and the remaining olive oil.

Bake 18 to 20 minutes, or until crust is medium brown. Slide the entire pissaladière onto a serving board and garnish with fresh herb sprigs. Or cut into squares and serve on a large platter.

HAM AND TURNIP GREENS SOUP WITH CORN BISCUIT DUMPLINGS

4 SERVINGS

I love to make this flavorful soup for dinner on a cold winter night. If you can't get fresh greens, add a 10-ounce package of frozen greens to the boiling liquid.

SOUP

1 *can (13¾ ounces) chicken or beef broth*

3 *cups water*

1 *bunch (about 14 ounces) turnip or mustard greens or kale*

1 *package (10 ounces) frozen black-eyed peas or baby lima beans (about 2 cups)*

1 *cup (6 ounces) diced smoked ham*

BISCUIT DUMPLINGS

⅓ *cup yellow cornmeal*

⅓ *cup all-purpose flour*

1 *teaspoon baking powder*

¼ *teaspoon salt*

1½ *tablespoons cold unsalted butter, cut up*

¼ *cup milk or broth*

To make soup, pour broth and water into a 5-quart pot and bring to a boil.

While the liquid comes to a boil, strip the leaves of the greens from the coarse stems. Discard the stems. Wash leaves, drain, and tear into pieces roughly 1 inch square (you should have 4 to 5 packed cups).

Add greens, black-eyed peas, and ham to boiling liquid. Cover the pot and simmer 5 to 6 minutes over moderately high heat while you make dumplings.

Mix cornmeal, flour, baking powder, and salt in a bowl. Add butter and rub in thoroughly with your fingers, until the mixture looks like fine granules. Add milk and stir with a fork until a soft, sticky dough forms.

Make sure the contents of the pot are simmering. Drop level tablespoons of dough ¼ inch apart on top of the soup. Cover and simmer over medium heat for 20 minutes (no looking), or until the dumplings appear dry on top. Makes about 8 dumplings, 7½ cups soup. The soup reheats well.

LAMB POTPIE PROVENÇALE

3 OR 4 SERVINGS

Rich and delicious and special enough for company. You might think of buying boneless lamb for this, but don't! The bones add flavor and help thicken the gravy.

STEW

- *3 thin strips bacon, diced, or 2 strips bacon, diced, and 1 tablespoon olive oil*
- *2 pounds lean lamb neck, or 2½ pounds lamb shanks cut into 2-inch lengths (I ask the butcher to do this)*
- *2 tablespoons all-purpose flour*
- *1 cup chopped onion*
- *1 cup coarsely chopped carrots*
- *1 cup (4 ounces) tiny whole mushrooms, or larger ones, quartered*
- *½ teaspoon each dried rosemary and thyme leaves*
- *1 cup dry red wine*
- *1 cup canned beef broth (not condensed), or water*

BISCUIT CRUST

- *1 cup all-purpose flour*
- *1½ teaspoons baking powder*
- *½ teaspoon salt*

3 tablespoons cold unsalted butter, cut up

⅓ cup milk or beef broth

To prepare stew, fry bacon in a 9- to 10-inch skillet over medium heat about 5 minutes, or until the bacon is light brown and plenty of fat has come out. With a slotted spoon, transfer the bacon to a 2- to 2½-quart ovenproof casserole, about 8 inches in diameter. Roll half the lamb in flour, shaking off excess, and brown on both sides in bacon fat about 5 minutes; add to the casserole. Repeat with remaining meat. Add onions and carrots to the skillet and cook slowly 5 to 10 minutes, stirring now and then, until lightly browned.

Heat oven to 300° F. Sprinkle mushrooms, herbs, and browned vegetables over the meat. Add wine and broth to the skillet. Bring to a full rolling boil, stirring to incorporate any browned bits from skillet. Pour over the meat. Cover tightly with a lid or aluminum foil. Bake 1½ hours, or until the meat is tender.

While the meat is in the oven, start the crust. Mix flour, baking powder, and salt in a medium-size bowl. Add butter; cut in with a pastry blender or rub in with your fingers. (This much can be done ahead.) Remove stew from the oven and uncover; turn oven to 425° F. Add milk or broth to flour mixture and stir with a fork until a soft dough forms. Turn out dough onto a lightly floured surface and give 10 to 12 kneads. Turn smooth side up. Roll or pat to about 8 inches in diameter (to fit just inside casserole). Place dough on top of the stew (there should be lots of gravy). Bake, uncovered, about 20 minutes, or until the crust is medium brown. Lift an edge of the crust to check that the underside is cooked. Serve hot.

PEGGY'S CHEESE SCONES

My aunt likes to serve these (and we all love to eat them) for a summer supper, with thinly sliced cold roast beef or chicken and marinated tomatoes. Make the salad while the scones bake and let both stand for at least 3 hours so the flavors can develop. If you can get English Cheddar, you can omit the Parmesan.

1½ cups all-purpose flour

1½ teaspoons cream of tartar (see note)

½ teaspoon baking soda (see note)

1 teaspoon dry mustard

½ teaspoon salt

4 tablespoons (½ stick) cold unsalted butter or margarine (Peggy uses margarine), cut up

1 cup (4 ounces) shredded sharp Cheddar cheese

2 tablespoons grated Parmesan cheese

1 large egg

½ cup milk

Heat oven to 400° F. Put flour, cream of tartar, baking soda, dry mustard, and salt into a large bowl; mix well.

Add butter and cut in with a pastry blender or rub in with your fingers, until the mixture looks like fine granules. Add cheeses and toss to mix.

Break egg into milk and beat with a fork to blend well. Pour this over flour mixture and stir with a fork until a dough forms.

Turn out dough onto a lightly floured board and give 10 to 12 kneads. Cut dough in half. Knead each half briefly into a ball, turn smooth side up, and pat or roll into a 6-inch circle. Cut each circle into 6 wedges. Place on an ungreased cookie sheet.

Bake 12 to 15 minutes, or until medium brown. Cool, loosely wrapped in a dish towel, on a wire rack.

NOTE: Instead of the cream of tartar and baking soda you can use 1½ teaspoons baking powder.

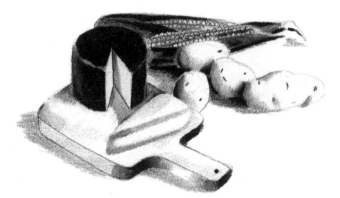

POTATO-ONION FLAT PIE

6 TO 8 SIDE-DISH
OR 2 TO 3 MAIN-DISH SERVINGS

Good as a side dish with roast beef or lamb, or with sautéed liver. Served with a crunchy salad, it makes a comforting main dish.

FILLING

2 tablespoons unsalted butter or margarine

1 tablespoon olive or vegetable oil

1½ cups sliced onions (8 ounces whole onions)

1 pound all-purpose potatoes, scrubbed but not peeled, sliced ⅛ inch thick (2 to 2¼ cups)

½ teaspoon salt

½ teaspoon pepper

⅓ cup light cream or half-and-half

BISCUIT CRUST

1 cup all-purpose flour

1½ teaspoons baking powder

½ teaspoon cracked black pepper, or ¼ teaspoon regular ground pepper

½ teaspoon salt

2½ tablespoons cold unsalted butter, cut up

⅓ cup chicken broth or milk

To make filling, heat butter and oil in a 10- to 12-inch skillet over medium heat. Stir in onions, cover, and cook about 5 minutes, stirring once, until wilted. Stir in potatoes and sprinkle with salt and pepper. Cover and cook 10 minutes more over medium-low heat, stirring or shaking three or four times, until potatoes are translucent and onions golden.

Meanwhile, heat oven to 400° F. To make crust, mix flour, baking powder, cracked pepper, and salt in a large bowl. Add butter and cut in with a pastry blender or rub in with your fingers, until the mixture looks like fine granules. Add chicken broth; stir with a fork until the mixture forms a soft dough.

Turn out dough onto a lightly floured surface and give 10 to 12 kneads. Turn smooth side up. Roll with a rolling pin into a 14-inch circle. Fold the dough over the rolling pin and lift onto a jelly-roll or pizza pan; open into a circle and patch any tears.

Spoon the potato mixture over the crust, leaving a 1½-inch border. Fold the border over the edge of the filling. Brush the border with 2 tablespoons of the cream. Bake 15 minutes. Pour the remaining cream over the potato filling. Bake 10 minutes longer, or until the crust is golden. Serve warm or at room temperature.

....
VARIATIONS

Samosa Flat Pie. Samosa flavor without the usual deep-frying. Add 1 to 2 teaspoons curry powder to onions just before adding potatoes. About 3 minutes before potatoes are cooked, add 1 cup frozen green peas to skillet. Serve the pie with plain yogurt flavored with chopped fresh coriander and chopped peeled cucumber.

French Country Pie. Add 1 cup coarsely grated Emmentaler or Gruyère cheese to the cooked potato mixture.

CANADIAN PORK PIE

6 MAIN-DISH SERVINGS

This Canadian meat pie is usually made with pie crust. I prefer this biscuit crust because it is easier and uses a lot less fat.

FILLING

1 *pound ground lean pork or beef*

1 *cup chopped onion*

1 *teaspoon dried thyme leaves, crumbled*

1/2 *teaspoon salt*

1/2 *teaspoon ground allspice or nutmeg*

1/4 *teaspoon pepper*

BISCUIT CRUST

1 1/2 *cups all-purpose flour*

2 *teaspoons baking powder*

1 *teaspoon salt*

1/2 *teaspoon dried thyme leaves, crumbled*

1/4 *teaspoon ground allspice or nutmeg*

3 *tablespoons solid vegetable shortening (or butter or margarine)*

1/2 *cup plus 1 tablespoon milk or chicken broth*

GLAZE

1 *whole egg or 1 egg yolk beaten with 2 tablespoons water (optional)*

To make filling, cook meat and onion in an 8- to 10-inch skillet over medium heat 8 to 10 minutes, mashing meat frequently with the back of a spoon so that it becomes quite crumbly. Sprinkle meat with thyme, salt, allspice, and pepper as it cooks. When the onion is lightly browned and the meat has lost its pink color, remove from heat. If there's more than 1 tablespoon of fat in the skillet, spoon it off. Let the mixture cool to lukewarm in the skillet or on a plate.

While meat cools, check that one rack is in the bottom third of oven and heat oven to 425° F. To make crust, put flour, baking powder, salt, thyme, and allspice in a medium-size bowl; stir to mix well. Add shortening and cut in with a pastry blender or rub in with your fingers, until the mixture looks slightly damp and the shortening is in lumps about the size of small peas. Add milk and stir with a fork until a firm dough forms. Turn out dough onto a lightly floured surface and give 10 to 12 kneads. Cut in half. Knead one half briefly, turn smooth side up, and roll out about ½ inch wider than a 9-inch pie pan. Line the pan with dough and spread filling evenly in it. Wet the edges of the crust with your fingers or a brush dipped in water.

Knead and roll out remaining dough the same way and place on top of meat. Press edges of crust together and trim off dough extending beyond edge of pie pan. Cut four 2-inch slits in top crust so steam can escape. Brush with glaze. Bake 20 minutes, or until golden brown on top; cover the top loosely with foil and bake 10 minutes more. Cool 10 minutes before serving. Cut into wedges.

FRESH HERB–OLIVE OIL SCONES

The secret to delicious herb scones is not to go wild with the herbs but to choose them wisely. To the base of basil and green onions or chives, add one strong flavor such as marjoram, thyme, or oregano. Mint is not good, neither are very woody herbs such as rosemary.

- **2 cups all-purpose flour**
- **1 tablespoon baking powder**
- **¼ cup coarsely grated Parmesan cheese**
- **½ teaspoon salt**
- **¼ teaspoon freshly ground black pepper**
- **½ cup buttermilk or plain yogurt**
- **⅓ cup olive oil (extra-virgin, virgin, or light)**
- **1 large egg**
- **2 teaspoons lemon juice**
- **½ teaspoon minced fresh garlic**
- **2 tablespoons snipped chives, or the green part of green onions (scallions), thinly sliced**
- **1 tablespoon chopped fresh basil leaves**
- **1 teaspoon coarsely chopped fresh marjoram, thyme, or oregano leaves**

Heat oven to 375° F. Put flour, baking powder, Parmesan, salt, and pepper into a large bowl. Stir to mix well.

In another bowl, whisk buttermilk, oil, egg, lemon juice, garlic, chives, and herbs until well blended.

Scrape herb mixture into flour. Stir with a spoon until a soft dough forms.

Turn out dough onto a lightly floured board and give 10 to 15 kneads. Gather dough into a ball and cut in half. Place both halves on a cookie sheet and roll or pat each into an 8- to 9-inch round. Cut each circle into 8 wedges; do not separate wedges.

Bake 15 to 20 minutes or until lightly browned. Put on a wire rack to cool for 5 minutes. Wrap loosely in a dish towel on the rack and cool at least 15 to 20 minutes more before serving.

HOMEY DESSERTS

BEST BLUEBERRY COBBLER

Good with cream, yogurt, or vanilla ice cream. This recipe works well with both fresh and unsweetened frozen blueberries.

FILLING

4 *cups (2 pints) blueberries*
½ *cup seedless red raspberry jam*

BISCUIT TOPPING

1 *cup all-purpose flour*
1 *tablespoon granulated sugar*
1 *teaspoon baking powder*
⅛ *teaspoon salt*
3 *tablespoons cold unsalted butter, cut up*
½ *cup light cream or milk*

Heat oven to 425° F. Mix blueberries and jam in a round or square 8-inch baking dish. For frozen berries, put the dish in the oven while you make topping so berries thaw.

Mix flour, sugar, baking powder, and salt in a medium-size bowl. Cut in butter with a pastry blender or rub in with your fingers, until the mixture looks like fine granules.

Add cream and stir with a fork until a soft dough forms. Drop well-rounded tablespoons of dough on blueberries (about 10 tablespoons). Bake 25 to 30 minutes, or until the topping is brown and berries are bubbling around the edge. Let cool at least 10 minutes before serving.

BLUEBERRY-GRAPE SLUMP

6 SERVINGS

Here, the biscuits steam on top of the fruit, which gives them a lovely flavor. Grape juice brings out the best in blueberries. Try this easy skillet dessert after a roast chicken dinner.

FILLING

- *1 can (6 ounces) frozen concentrated sweetened Concord grape juice*
- *3 tablespoons water*
- *1 package (1 pound) frozen blueberries, or 3 to 3½ cups fresh blueberries*
- *1 teaspoon vanilla extract*

BISCUITS

- *¾ cup all-purpose flour*
- *¼ cup granulated sugar*
- *1 teaspoon baking powder*
- *¼ teaspoon salt*
- *1 tablespoon cold butter, cut up*
- *¼ cup milk*
- *½ teaspoon vanilla extract*
- *Nutmeg sugar, made by mixing 1 teaspoon granulated sugar and ⅛ teaspoon ground nutmeg*

To make filling, put grape juice concentrate into a 9- to 10-inch stainless or nonstick skillet, rinsing container with the water. Add blueberries and vanilla; bring to a simmer over moderately high heat. Let simmer, uncovered, about 5 minutes.

While the blueberries simmer, mix flour, sugar, baking powder, and salt in a large bowl. Add butter and rub in with your fingers until the butter is in tiny pieces.

Mix milk and vanilla; pour over the flour mixture. Stir with a fork to form a soft dough. Drop rounded teaspoons of dough (about 12) on top of the fruit, leaving space between. Cover and simmer 20 minutes over low heat, or until the swollen dumplings look dry on the top, spring back when gently pressed, and are cooked through. Remove from heat, sprinkle with nutmeg sugar, and serve warm.

ELLEN LANSING'S
STRAWBERRY SHORTCAKES

6 SHORTCAKES

According to my husband, a great strawberry shortcake is made up of the following, assembled with a generous hand: a hot, unsweetened baking powder biscuit, juicy room-temperature berries, and very cold, sweetened whipped cream. The plain biscuits should have a slightly acid aftertaste and contrast with the berries and cream. Serve these after a light main course or, even better, as a glorious treat on a midsummer afternoon.

> **6 Good-with-Anything Baking Powder Biscuits
> (page 16)**
> **1 quart (1½ pounds) ripe strawberries**
> **3 tablespoons granulated sugar, or to taste**
> **1 cup whipping cream**
> **Soft butter, if desired**

The biscuits can be baked at the last minute, or they may be baked ahead and warmed just before serving.

One to two hours before serving, rinse and hull the berries. Slice about one quarter of them into a bowl. Sprinkle with 2 tablespoons of sugar and mash lightly with a fork to get the juices flowing. Slice and add the remaining berries; mix gently. Let stand 1 hour at room temperature, or cover and refrigerate for longer, but bring to room temperature before serving. (Taste berries shortly before serving and add more sugar if needed.)

Add the remaining tablespoon of sugar to the cream and whip until soft peaks form when the beater is lifted. Cover the cream and refrigerate until needed. The cream may "water out" on standing, but can be rewhipped briefly at the last minute.

To serve, pull biscuits apart, butter them if you wish, and put the bottom halves on serving plates. Spoon about ¼ cup berries and some of the juice over each. Crown with about ¼ cup whipped cream and then the biscuit top. Spoon over the remaining berries and cream.

NOTE: See Shortcake Tips, page 60.

....

VARIATION

Sadie Spratley's Southern Strawberry Shortcakes. Southerners like Mrs. Spratley generally prefer a sweeter shortcake. Follow above directions but use Simple Sweet Scones (page 76) instead of baking powder biscuits.

SINFULLY DELICIOUS CARAMEL-BANANA SHORTCAKES

For best flavor, choose ripe bananas with speckled skins. And look in specialty food shops for a wonderful butterscotch-caramel fudge topping that's perfect for this treat.

1 cup whipping cream

½ cup (approximately) butterscotch or caramel sauce (homemade or purchased)

6 warm Good-with-Anything Baking Powder Biscuits (page 16)

2 large or 3 medium-size bananas

Mix cream and ¼ cup of butterscotch or caramel sauce in a small bowl. Whip with an electric or rotary beater until soft peaks form when the beater is lifted.

Split biscuits and put bottoms on individual serving plates. Spoon about ¼ cup of cream mixture over each. Slice the bananas onto the cream, saving a few slices for garnish. Put tops back on biscuits. Spoon remaining cream over. Add reserved banana slices and drizzle a generous teaspoon of sauce over each serving.

NOTE: See Shortcake Tips, page 60.

SUMMER FRUIT SHORTCAKES

12 SHORTCAKES

1 pint ripe strawberries

2 tablespoons plus 2 teaspoons granulated sugar, or to taste

2 cups fresh or frozen blueberries or blackberries

2 large ripe peaches

2 cups whipping cream

12 warm Simple Sweet Scones (page 76), made with ⅓ cup sugar, or Good-with-Anything Baking Powder Biscuits (page 16)

Rinse and hull the strawberries. Slice about 1 cup of them into a bowl; add 2 teaspoons of sugar and mash lightly. Slice and add remaining strawberries. Add the blueberries; mix gently. Slice the peaches into the bowl, pulling off the skin as you go. (Skin should easily come off really ripe peaches.) Mix the fruit gently. Let stand 1 hour at room temperature. Taste the fruit after about half an hour; add more sugar if needed. (The fruit may now be refrigerated.)

Whip the cream with the remaining 2 tablespoons of sugar until soft peaks form when the beater is lifted.

To serve, split the scones apart and put the bottom halves on serving plates. Spoon about ¼ cup fruit and ¼ cup whipped cream over each. Cover with the scone top and finish with a little more fruit and cream.

NOTE: See Shortcake Tips, page 60.

ALMOND-GRAPE SHORTCAKE

6 TO 8 SERVINGS

Threader he almond shortcake is quickly made in a blender or food processor and baked in a cake pan. I like to decorate the cake with scented geranium leaves from the pots on my window ledge.

½ cup granulated sugar

½ cup almonds (I use the whole unblanched nuts, but whatever you have on hand will do just fine)

1 large egg

1 teaspoon almond extract

⅓ cup milk or cream

4 tablespoons (½ stick) cold unsalted butter, cut up

1 teaspoon baking powder

1 cup all-purpose flour

1 cup whipping cream, whipped stiff with 1 teaspoon sugar

1 pound seedless green grapes, rinsed and halved (or 2 cups raspberries or blackberries, sliced peaches, or sliced kiwi and diced mango)

Heat oven to 350° F. Butter an 8-inch layer cake pan or, in a pinch, a pie pan.

Put sugar into a blender. With the machine running on medium speed, drop in almonds a few at a time. When thoroughly ground, drop in egg and almond extract. Pour in milk. Stop the machine and scrape down the sides. With the machine running, drop in butter, about 1 tablespoon at a time. Add baking powder. Stop the machine and scrape sides. Add ⅓ cup of the flour. Replace the blender cover; run the machine on low for a few seconds. Stop and scrape the sides. Add remaining flour the same way, blending only until flour is thoroughly mixed in.

Spread batter evenly in the prepared pan. Bake 30 minutes or until pale gold tinged with brown. Place the pan on a wire rack. Cool about 5 minutes, then turn the cake out onto the rack.

Cut shortcake into wedges. Serve each wedge topped with a spoonful of whipped cream and some of the fruit. Shortcake can be served warm or cold.

SHORTCAKE TIPS

I f you're making shortcakes for a large party, allow ⅓ cup whipped cream and ⅓ cup fruit to fill each generously. Cream doubles in volume when whipped (½ pint unwhipped cream makes 1 pint, or 2 cups, whipped).

Two-inch biscuits are large enough for dessert after a fairly filling main course or for an afternoon tea. For larger biscuits, use a 2½-inch cutter; the above amounts of fruit and cream will be sufficient.

WHIPPING CREAM

Cream whips fastest when very cold. In hot weather, chill both the mixing bowl and the beaters. Use an electric mixer or rotary beater. If using a rotary beater, choose a deep narrow bowl (rather than a wide, shallow one) so cream doesn't splash everywhere and maintains close contact with the beaters. Put a damp cloth on the table under the bowl to keep it steady. Watch the cream carefully as you whip and stop when it is billowy, well before it begins to look grainy or curdled. However, should the cream curdle, add a little more unwhipped cream and whip again, watching more carefully.

DRIED FRUIT BISCUIT STRUDEL

8 TO 10 SERVINGS

I love this for any festive fall or winter occasion. The biscuit crust is faster to work with than the more commonly used phyllo leaves. If you like, sift a little confectioners' sugar over the top before serving. The recipe reads long but goes together quickly.

BISCUIT CRUST

 1/3 **cup milk**

  2 **tablespoons granulated sugar**

1 1/4 **cups all-purpose flour**

1 1/2 **teaspoons baking powder**

 1/4 **teaspoon salt**

  4 **tablespoons (1/2 stick) cold unsalted butter, cut up**

FILLING

  1 **package (11 ounces) diced, mixed dried fruit, or 1 package (11 ounces) mixed whole dried fruit plus 1/2 cup golden raisins or Zante currants**

 1/4 **cup sweet orange marmalade, or peach or apricot preserves**

  2 **tablespoons freshly squeezed lemon juice, or 1/4 cup port or dry sherry wine**

 1/2 **teaspoon freshly grated orange peel (optional)**

CRUMB MIXTURE

¼ *cup walnuts, finely chopped*

3 *tablespoons granulated sugar*

3 *tablespoons plain, packaged dried bread crumbs*

½ *teaspoon ground cinnamon*

To make crust, measure milk and stir in sugar. Mix flour, baking powder, and salt in a large bowl. Add butter and cut in with a pastry blender or rub in with your fingers, until the mixture looks like fine granules. Stir milk and pour over the flour mixture. Stir with a fork until a dough forms. Turn out onto a lightly floured surface and give 10 to 15 kneads. Turn dough over and pat into a rectangle. Cover loosely and refrigerate while you prepare the filling.

If using whole dried fruit, cut into small pieces (⅛ to ¼ inch) with scissors, discarding prune pits. Mix all filling ingredients in a bowl.

To make crumb mixture, mix together all ingredients.

Check that one rack is in the top third of the oven and heat oven to 425° F. On a lightly floured surface, roll dough to a 15 × 12-inch rectangle with the 15-inch sides facing you. Make sure the dough is not stuck to the surface. (If it is, loosen with a metal spatula and flour the surface lightly.) Sprinkle ⅓ cup of the crumb mixture over the dough, leaving 1-inch borders on the two shorter sides, a 1½-inch border on the side closest to you, and a 3-inch border on the side farthest from you. Spoon fruit evenly over crumbs and top with remaining crumbs. Moisten the 3-inch border with a pastry brush or your finger dipped in water. Roll up dough, starting from the edge nearest you.

Put the roll seam side down on an ungreased cookie sheet.

Bake 10 minutes. Turn heat down to 325° F. and bake 20 to 25 minutes longer, or until pale brown and dry-looking. After 15 minutes, if strudel seems to be browning very fast, cover loosely with foil. Carefully transfer baked strudel to a wire rack. Cool at least 1 hour before serving. Trim the ends on the diagonal; cut the strudel into 8 to 10 diagonal slices.

LEMON-ROSEMARY APPLE PANDOWDY

6 SERVINGS

Pandowdies, cobblers, slumps, and grunts are all variations on biscuit dough cooked with fruit. These down-home desserts from early New England are enjoying a welcome revival. Try this refreshing pandowdy after a rich soup or stew.

FILLING

½ *teaspoon dried rosemary leaves*

⅓ *cup granulated sugar*

2 *tablespoons freshly squeezed lemon juice*

1½ *pounds Golden Delicious apples, peeled, quartered, cored, and thinly sliced (5 cups)*

BISCUIT TOPPING

1 *cup all-purpose flour*

1 *tablespoon granulated sugar*

1 *teaspoon baking powder*

⅛ *teaspoon salt*

½ *teaspoon dried rosemary leaves*

3 *tablespoons cold unsalted butter, cut up*

⅓ *cup light cream or milk*

Heat oven to 425° F. Have ready a heavy baking dish about 8 inches square or round.

To make filling, crumble rosemary as fine as possible

into a bowl. Add sugar and lemon juice; stir. Add apple slices; toss to coat. Spread evenly in the baking dish.

To make biscuit topping, put flour, sugar, baking powder, salt, and rosemary into a medium-size bowl, crumbling the rosemary as fine as possible. Add butter and cut in with a pastry blender or rub in with your fingers, until the mixture looks like fine granules.

Add cream. Stir with a fork until a soft dough forms. Turn out dough onto a lightly floured surface and give 10 to 12 kneads. Turn dough over and roll or pat to fit just inside the baking dish. Place on top of the fruit. Cut 4 slits in the dough so steam can escape.

Bake 25 to 30 minutes, or until the crust is golden. With a knife, lift edge of crust and make sure it is cooked underneath. Remove from the oven. Serve warm.

COFFEE AND TEATIME TREATS

GINGERBREAD SCONES

Delicious with honey anytime, or with Cheddar cheese for lunch. Excellent, too, with sliced bananas and whipped cream for tea or dessert.

⅓ cup milk

⅓ cup light molasses

2 cups all-purpose flour

2 teaspoons baking powder

¼ teaspoon baking soda

1 teaspoon ground cinnamon

1 teaspoon ground ginger

¼ teaspoon ground cloves

7 tablespoons cold unsalted butter, cut up

Heat oven to 425° F. Measure milk in a glass cup measure; add molasses to the ⅔ cup mark and stir to blend.

Mix dry ingredients in a large bowl. Add butter and cut in with a pastry blender or rub in with your fingers, until mixture looks like fine granules. Stir milk mixture and add. Stir with a fork to form a smooth, rather soft dough.

Turn out dough onto a lightly floured surface and give 10 to 12 kneads. Cut dough in half. Knead each half briefly into a ball, turn smooth side up, and place on an ungreased cookie sheet. Pat each piece of dough into a 5-inch circle; cut into 6 or 8 wedges; leave sides touching. Bake about 10 minutes, or until medium brown. Do not overbake. Cool, loosely wrapped in a cloth, on a wire rack.

CHOCOLATE-CHIP
SCONES FROM PLUMS

12 SCONES

When I'm feeling very self-indulgent, on my way to work I stop at Plums, a pretty outdoor café (owned by Richard Lavin of Sofi's and Lavin's restaurants) in New York City. There I pick up a container of cappuccino and one of these incredibly delectable scones. Rich and crumbly, they were developed by the chef, Kevin O'Brien.

3 cups all-purpose flour

1 tablespoon baking powder

½ pound (2 sticks) unsalted butter, at room temperature

¼ cup plus 2 tablespoons granulated sugar

3 large eggs

⅓ cup buttermilk or plain yogurt

½ cup semisweet chocolate chips

Mix flour and baking powder in a bowl. In the large bowl of an electric mixer, beat butter on high speed until creamy. Add sugar and beat 3 to 5 minutes until pale and fluffy. Add eggs, one at a time, beating after each.

Scrape sides of bowl; reduce speed to low. Add flour mixture; mix only until blended. Scrape sides; add buttermilk and mix only until blended. Remove the bowl from the machine. Sprinkle chocolate chips over the batter and fold in.

Scoop ⅓ cupfuls of dough onto an ungreased cookie sheet, placing the mounds about 2 inches apart. (An ice-cream scoop speeds scooping.)

Loosely cover dough with plastic wrap and refrigerate about 45 minutes (or freeze, and when hard, remove to a plastic bag and freeze for up to 6 weeks).

Heat oven to 350° F. Uncover scones and bake 15 minutes. Turn heat down to 325° F. and bake about 13 minutes longer, or until pale golden brown. Cool, uncovered, on a wire rack.

COFFEE-HAZELNUT SCONES

14 SCONES

> **1 cup hazelnuts (also known as filberts)**
> **1 cup milk**
> **2 tablespoons instant coffee granules**
> **2½ cups all-purpose flour**
> **1 tablespoon baking powder**
> **½ teaspoon salt**
> **8 tablespoons (1 stick) cold unsalted butter, cut up**
> **⅔ cup packed brown sugar**

Heat oven to 350° F. Put hazelnuts in a pie pan (or any baking pan with sides) and bake 15 to 20 minutes, shaking the pan once or twice, until skins split and nuts are lightly browned. Pour the nuts onto a dish towel; gather the towel around the nuts, and rub them hard through the towel for a minute or so to loosen the skins. Pick out nuts (some stubborn skins will remain) and coarsely chop in a food processor or by hand with a chef's knife. Turn oven up to 425° F.

While nuts are toasting, measure milk and stir in instant coffee. Put flour, baking powder, and salt into a large bowl; stir to mix well. Add butter and cut in with a pastry blender or rub in with your fingers, until the mixture looks like fine granules.

Add sugar and hazelnuts; toss to distribute evenly. Stir milk mixture, pour into the bowl, and stir with a wooden spoon until a soft dough forms.

Scoop ¼ cupfuls of dough and place about 2 inches apart onto an ungreased cookie sheet. Bake about 15 minutes, or until the dough colors but does not get dark brown. Put scones on a dish towel on a wire rack; cover loosely with the cloth and cool 1 to 2 hours before serving.

APRICOT SWIRL SCONES

12 SCONES

As good for breakfast as they are for tea. You may omit the prebaking refrigeration, although it does produce a finer texture and more intense apricot flavor. For a festive occasion, sprinkle the unbaked scones with ¼ cup chopped pistachios once they are on the cookie sheet.

FILLING

- ¾ cup (4 ounces) dried apricots
- 2 tablespoons honey
- 2 2-inch strips lemon peel, removed with a vegetable peeler
- 1 tablespoon lemon juice

DOUGH

- 3 cups all-purpose flour
- 1 tablespoon baking powder
- ¼ teaspoon salt
- ½ pound (2 sticks) unsalted butter, at room temperature
- ¼ cup granulated sugar
- 3 large eggs
- 1 teaspoon vanilla extract
- ⅓ cup buttermilk or plain yogurt

Finely chop the apricots and put into a small saucepan with remaining filling ingredients. Add ¼ cup water. Cover and simmer 10 minutes over low heat until apricots are very soft. Discard lemon peel. Mash apricots with the back of a spoon to a coarse, thick puree.

While the filling cooks, mix flour, baking powder, and salt in a bowl. In the large bowl of an electric mixer, beat butter on medium speed until creamy. Add sugar and beat 2 to 3 minutes, until pale and fluffy. Add eggs, one at a time, beating after each. Beat in vanilla.

Scrape sides of bowl; reduce speed to low. Add flour mixture; beat only until blended. Scrape sides; add buttermilk and mix only until blended.

Remove bowl from the machine. Fold apricot puree into the batter with a rubber spatula just until the puree is swirled through.

Scoop ⅓ cupfuls of dough onto an ungreased cookie sheet, placing the mounds about 2 inches apart. Loosely cover with plastic wrap and refrigerate about 45 minutes (or freeze and, when hard, remove to a plastic bag and freeze for up to 6 weeks).

Heat oven to 350° F. Uncover scones and bake 15 minutes. Turn heat down to 325° F. and bake 10 to 13 minutes longer, or until pale golden brown. Cool, uncovered, on a wire rack.

WELSH CURRANT SCONES

....

18 TRIANGULAR SCONES

These delicate, lightly spiced scones are baked range-top or in an electric skillet, which means you can have them on the table in less than 20 minutes since there's no oven to heat.

> **2 cups all-purpose flour**
>
> **1/3 cup granulated sugar; increase to 1/2 cup if a sweeter scone is desired**
>
> **1 teaspoon baking powder**
>
> **1/2 teaspoon salt**
>
> **1/2 teaspoon ground nutmeg**
>
> **1/2 cup solid vegetable shortening**
>
> **4 tablespoons (1/2 stick) cold unsalted butter, cut up**
>
> **1/2 cup Zante currants or dark raisins**
>
> **1 large egg**
>
> **1/3 cup milk**

Start heating an electric skillet to 325° F. or heat a griddle or heavy skillet over medium-low heat.

Put flour, sugar, baking powder, salt, and nutmeg into a large bowl; stir to mix well. Add shortening and butter and cut in with a pastry blender or rub in with your fingers, until mixture looks like fine granules.

Add currants; toss to distribute evenly.

Beat egg and milk with a fork to blend. Pour over the

flour mixture and stir with the fork until a soft dough forms.

Turn out dough onto a lightly floured surface and give 10 to 12 kneads. Cut dough into thirds. Roll or pat each piece into a 6-inch circle and cut into 6 wedges.

Place wedges apart in the heated skillet. Bake uncovered, 3 to 5 minutes per side, turning once, until medium brown. Serve right away, or cool, loosely covered with a cloth, on a wire rack.

SIMPLE SWEET SCONES

Mildly sweet and delicious anytime with butter and honey or preserves. Strawberry, plum, and black currant are three of my favorites.

2½ cups all-purpose flour

1 tablespoon baking powder

½ teaspoon salt

8 tablespoons (1 stick) cold unsalted butter, cut up

¼ cup granulated sugar (use ⅓ cup for slightly sweeter scones)

⅔ cup milk

Heat oven to 425° F. Put flour, baking powder, and salt into a large bowl; stir to mix well.

Add butter and cut in with a pastry blender or rub in with your fingers, until the mixture looks like fine granules. Add sugar; toss to mix.

Add milk and stir with a fork until a soft dough forms. Form dough into a ball, put onto a lightly floured board, and give 10 to 12 kneads.

To make triangular scones, cut dough in half. Knead each half lightly into a ball and turn smooth side up. Pat or roll into a 6-inch circle. Cut each circle into 6 or 8 wedges. Place wedges on an ungreased cookie sheet—slightly apart for crisp sides, touching for soft sides.

Bake about 12 minutes, or until medium brown on top. Put on a linen or cotton dish towel on a wire rack; cover loosely with the cloth and cool completely before serving.

NOTE: To make round scones with a 2-inch cutter, roll out dough to about $12 \times 5\frac{1}{2}$ inches. Cut out 15 scones. Reroll and cut scraps. For a $2\frac{1}{2}$-inch cutter, roll dough about $14 \times 5\frac{1}{2}$ inches and cut out 10 scones; reroll and cut scraps.

....
VARIATIONS

Sweet Whole-Wheat Scones. Omit $1\frac{1}{2}$ cups of the all-purpose flour and substitute $1\frac{1}{2}$ cups whole-wheat flour. Cut as for Simple Sweet Scones. Bake at 375° F. about 15 minutes.

Lemon Scones. Add 1 tablespoon freshly grated lemon peel to flour mixture. In a small bowl, mix 2 teaspoons fresh lemon juice with 2 tablespoons sugar; top each scone with $\frac{1}{4}$ teaspoonful before baking.

Lavender Scones. In a small saucepan over medium heat, bring milk and 1 tablespoon dried lavender flowers just to a boil. Cool to lukewarm. Strain into a measuring cup; add more milk if needed to measure $\frac{2}{3}$ cup. Substitute for the liquid in Simple Sweet Scones recipe. Lavender Scones are delicious plain, or filled with whipped cream and sliced peaches or halved green grapes.

Scented Geranium Scones. Add 4 or 5 very finely chopped scented geranium leaves (do not use regular geranium leaves) with the sugar. Or, if using a food processor, chop the leaves with the flour before adding butter.

CINNAMON BISCUIT CRISPS

40 CRISPS

These are very special: wafer-thin whole-wheat biscuits topped with cinnamon sugar. Delicious with a fruit compote or with hot chocolate or a glass of lemonade. They also keep well, if given the opportunity!

1½ cups whole-wheat flour

1 cup all-purpose flour

1 tablespoon baking powder

½ teaspoon salt

2 teaspoons ground cinnamon

8 tablespoons (1 stick) cold unsalted butter, cut up

¼ cup plus 2 tablespoons granulated sugar

⅔ cup milk

Heat oven to 400° F. Put flours, baking powder, salt, and ½ teaspoon cinnamon into a large bowl; stir to mix well.

Add butter and cut in with a pastry blender or rub in with your fingers, until the mixture looks like fine granules. Add 2 tablespoons of the sugar and toss to mix.

Add milk and stir with a fork until the mixture forms a dough. Gather into a ball; put onto a lightly floured board and give 10 to 12 kneads. Cut dough in half.

Mix the remaining ¼ cup sugar and remaining 1½ teaspoons cinnamon in a small bowl.

On a lightly floured board, roll out half the dough into a 7 × 6-inch rectangle. Lift dough and sprinkle the board with half the cinnamon sugar. Roll dough on the sugar (without turning dough over) into a rectangle about 14 × 11 inches. Trim the edges. Cut dough in 4 lengthwise strips, then 5 crosswise ones to make 20 rectangles. Put the rectangles, sugar side up, an inch or so apart on ungreased cookie sheets (nonstick work best).

Bake 7 to 10 minutes or until medium brown on top; watch that undersides do not scorch. Cool, uncovered, on a wire rack.

Roll, cut, and bake remaining dough. Bake the trimmings too—they are the cook's perk. Store airtight at room temperature.

....
VARIATION

Crisp Cinnamon Rounds. Roll each half of dough into a 16-inch circle and cut out with a plain, round 3- or 4-inch cutter. Bake as above. Makes about 40.

SWEET BARLEY DROP SCONES

Crumblier than a scone made entirely with all-purpose wheat flour. The barley flour (which you can buy in a health food store) adds a delicious flavor and whole-grain nutrition. Good with butter for breakfast as well as with afternoon coffee or tea.

1½ cups barley flour

1 cup all-purpose flour

1 tablespoon baking powder

½ teaspoon salt

8 tablespoons (1 stick) cold unsalted butter, cut up

¼ cup granulated sugar (use ⅓ cup for a slightly sweeter scone)

⅔ cup milk

Heat oven to 375° F. Put flours, baking powder, and salt into a large bowl; stir to mix well.

Add butter and cut in with a pastry blender or rub in with your fingers, until mixture looks like fine granules.

Add sugar; toss to mix. Add milk and stir with a fork until a wet dough forms. Drop rounded tablespoons of dough on an ungreased cookie sheet, placing mounds about 2 inches apart.

Bake about 15 minutes, or until pale golden brown. Cool on a wire rack.

Sweet Oat Drop Scones. Instead of barley flour use 2 cups old-fashioned oats ground fine in a blender or food processor. (You can buy oat flour but home-ground oats have a better flavor.)

Simple Sweet Drop Scones. Omit barley flour; use 2½ cups all-purpose flour and 1 cup milk. Drop ¼ cupfuls of the dough about 2 inches apart. Bake at 350° F. for 20 to 25 minutes, or until lightly browned. Makes about 12 scones.

ORANGE-ALMOND SCONES

Good just the way they are, warm and fragrant from the oven, or cooled for an hour or two. Or have them the next day.

1/2 cup freshly squeezed orange juice

1/4 cup buttermilk, plain yogurt, or milk

1 large egg

1/4 teaspoon almond extract

3 cups all-purpose flour

4 teaspoons baking powder

1/2 teaspoon baking soda

1/4 teaspoon salt

8 tablespoons (1 stick) cold unsalted butter, cut up

1/2 cup granulated sugar

1/2 cup finely chopped blanched almonds

1 tablespoon freshly grated orange peel

Heat oven to 375° F. Grate the peel before juicing the orange. Measure juice, then buttermilk in a 2-cup glass measure. Add egg and extract; beat smooth with a fork.

Put flour, baking powder, baking soda, and salt into a large bowl. Stir to mix well. Add butter and cut in with a pastry blender or rub in with your fingers, until the mixture looks like fine granules. Add sugar, almonds, and orange peel; toss to distribute evenly. Add egg mixture and stir with a fork until a soft dough forms.

Turn out dough onto a lightly floured board and give 5 to 6 kneads, just until well mixed. Form dough into a ball; cut into 8 wedges. Form each wedge into a ball and place on an ungreased cookie sheet.

Bake about 25 minutes, or until medium brown. Cool on a wire rack.

HAMANTASCHEN

....

The origin and meaning of the name may be disputed but not the delicious flavor of this traditional Purim sweet. They may be frozen before baking.

2½ cups all-purpose flour

1 tablespoon baking powder

½ teaspoon ground cinnamon (optional)

½ teaspoon salt

8 tablespoons (1 stick) cold unsalted butter, cut up, or ½ cup vegetable shortening

⅓ cup granulated sugar

⅔ cup milk

1 cup (approximately) prune butter, or poppy seed filling (see note)

Heat oven to 350° F. Put flour, baking powder, cinnamon, and salt into a large bowl; stir to mix well. Add butter and cut in with a pastry blender or rub in with your fingers, until the mixture looks like fine granules. Add sugar; toss to distribute. Add milk and stir with a fork until a soft dough forms.

Turn out dough onto a lightly floured surface and give 10 to 12 kneads. Cut dough in half. Knead each half briefly into a ball, then turn smooth side up. Roll out on a lightly floured surface into a 15-inch circle. Cut out dough with a plain 3-inch round cutter. Reroll and cut the scraps. Put ½ teaspoon prune butter in the middle of each circle. Wet the pastry around the filling with your finger or a brush dipped in cold water. Fold dough over in thirds and pinch edges firmly together to form a triangle.

Put the pastries on an ungreased cookie sheet and bake 12 to 15 minutes, or until very light brown. Cool, uncovered, on a wire rack. Store airtight.

NOTE: Look for prune butter in the jams and jellies section of your supermarket and poppy seed filling near the pie fillings or in the baking section.

A DEVONSHIRE CREAM TEA

This English teatime treat is perfect to share with friends on a relaxed summer afternoon. For a more substantial tea, add very thin tomato, ham, or cucumber sandwiches on buttered white bread, a cake or cookies, and steaming pots of Earl Grey tea. (Iced tea or coffee would be wonderful, too.) When we enjoyed a cream tea as children, the scones, clotted cream, butter, and jam were all made by Mother. Clotted cream, also called Devonshire or Cornish cream, needs thick, unpasteurized cream and lots of time. Crème Fraîche, homemade or purchased, is a very satisfactory substitute.

> *Simple Sweet Scones (page 76) or Good-with-Anything Baking Powder Biscuits (page 16)*
>
> *Strawberry Jam (recipe follows, or can be purchased)*
>
> *Crème Fraîche (purchased or homemade, see page 19), or lightly whipped cream*

Put the biscuits in a napkin-lined basket, the jam in one pretty glass bowl, the Crème Fraîche in another. Give each person a small plate (salad size is fine) and a knife. To eat, split a scone, spread each half with jam, top with cream and enjoy!

N O T E : Self-indulgent people like to butter the scone before spreading on the jam.

REFRIGERATOR
STRAWBERRY PRESERVES

....

1¼ CUPS

L emon juice and currant jelly give these preserves a
fresh, tart flavor. And you couldn't ask for an easier
way to prepare homemade jam.

½ cup red currant jelly

2 teaspoons freshly squeezed lemon juice

*1 pint small strawberries, rinsed, hulled, and
sliced*

Put jelly and lemon juice in a heavy, 4- to 5-quart pot with
a stainless or nonstick finish. Bring to a boil over high
heat, stirring to dissolve jelly. Boil 1 minute, or until large
bubbles appear and jelly is syrupy.

Stir in strawberries. Bring to a full rolling boil. Boil 1
minute. Remove from heat. Cover and let stand 5 minutes.
Mash berries with a fork. Pour mixture into a clean, dry jar
or into a refrigerator container. Let cool. Cover and store in
refrigerator up to 1 month.

APPETIZERS AND SAVORY SNACKS

BLACK PEPPER BISCUIT PRETZELS

32 SMALL PRETZELS

Quick to twist, these peppery hot snacks are good with a glass of ice-cold beer or a juice spritzer. They freeze well before baking.

2 cups all-purpose flour
1 tablespoon baking powder
2 teaspoons cracked black pepper
1 teaspoon salt
5 tablespoons cold unsalted butter, cut up
⅔ cup chicken broth

Heat oven to 450° F. Put flour, baking powder, pepper, and salt into a large bowl; stir to mix well.

Add butter and cut in with a pastry blender or rub in with your fingers, until the mixture looks like fine granules. Add chicken broth. Stir with a fork until the mixture clumps together to form a dough.

Turn out dough onto a lightly floured board and give 12 to 15 kneads. Shape into an 8-inch-long cylinder; cut into 8 equal pieces. Cut each piece into 4 smaller pieces; each will become a pretzel.

One at a time, roll each piece of dough with the palms of your hands to a 12-inch rope; twist into a pretzel shape and put on an ungreased cookie sheet.

Bake 5 minutes; turn pretzels over (use tongs or a towel) and bake about 3 minutes more, or until light brown. Cool pretzels, uncovered, on a wire rack.

FRESH HERB AND CHEESE
APPETIZER BISCUITS

For the pretty and flavorful fresh herb topping, mix two or three soft-leaved herbs such as oregano, chives, thyme, basil, chervil, and savory. Or try mixing one with about ½ cup basil—or use all basil. Leave the herbs in fairly big pieces.

1½ cups all-purpose flour

1½ teaspoons baking powder

½ teaspoon salt

4 tablespoons (½ stick) cold unsalted butter, cut up

1 large egg

½ cup milk

1 cup (4 ounces) shredded sharp Cheddar cheese

6 ounces whipped cream cheese, at room temperature

¾ cup chopped fresh herbs

Heat oven to 400° F. Put flour, baking powder, and salt into a large bowl; stir to mix well.

Add butter and cut in with a pastry blender or rub in with your fingers, until the mixture looks like fine granules.

Break the egg into the milk and beat with a fork until well blended. Pour over the flour mixture and stir with fork until a dough forms.

Turn out dough onto a lightly floured surface, sprinkle with Cheddar, and give 10 to 12 kneads; the cheese should remain visible. Form dough into a ball. Roll out to a ½- to ¾-inch-thick round. Cut with a 1½-inch plain biscuit cutter. Place on an ungreased cookie sheet and bake 10 to 13 minutes or until pale brown. Cool on a wire rack at least 10 minutes. If not to be used for several hours, store airtight.

Cut biscuits in half horizontally (a serrated knife works best). Work assembly-line fashion for speed: Spread each cut side with a little cream cheese. Then dip cream cheese in chopped fresh herbs. If desired, cover and refrigerate up to 6 hours; bring to room temperature before serving.

FRESH MUSHROOM APPETIZER PIE

8 TO 10 APPETIZER OR
2 TO 3 MAIN-DISH SERVINGS

A half-inch high, two-crust pie that's a cinch to make. It reheats well and bakes well from the frozen state, so why not make two and save one for later?

FILLING

8 ounces fresh mushrooms, cleaned

1 tablespoon unsalted butter

2 teaspoons all-purpose flour
   Freshly ground pepper, to taste

BISCUIT CRUST

1 cup all-purpose flour

1½ teaspoons baking powder

½ teaspoon salt

¼ cup olive oil

¼ cup milk or chicken broth

To make filling, finely chop mushrooms by hand or in food processor using on-off switch; you should have about 2 cups. Melt butter in a large skillet over medium heat. Add mushrooms and cook 5 to 7 minutes, stirring often, until any liquid has evaporated. Remove from heat; stir in flour and pepper. Spread the filling on a plate to cool quickly.

Heat oven to 425° F. To make the crust, mix flour, baking powder, and salt in a large bowl. Add olive oil and milk; stir to make a smooth, pasty dough. Cut dough in half. On an ungreased cookie sheet without sides, roll out one half the dough into a 9-inch circle (edges will be uneven). Put remaining dough between two sheets of wax paper and roll to a 9-inch circle.

Spread mushroom filling over dough on the cookie sheet to within 1 inch of the edge. Peel wax paper off the other circle of dough, lift bottom sheet, and flip dough over on top of the filling; peel off the wax paper.

Fold over the edges of dough and pat or crimp lightly. Cut four 2-inch slits in top so steam can escape. Bake 18 to 20 minutes, or until pale brown. Slide pie onto a wire rack; cool at least 10 minutes before serving.

PEGGY PRIMROSE ALSTON'S SUFFOLK RUSKS

24 RUSKS

At Christmas, my Aunt Peggy presents each member of the family with a big tin of these wonderful crunchy rusks—a welcome gift at a time of year when there's often a call for light meals. Basically these are dried biscuits, but as they dry they acquire a nutty flavor. The rusks are excellent with cheese for an appetizer; serve with grapes and apples for a snack, or with a bowl of soup for a light lunch. They will keep well for months.

> **2** cups all-purpose flour
> **1½** teaspoons cream of tartar (see note)
> **1** teaspoon baking soda
> **¼** teaspoon salt
> **6** tablespoons cold unsalted margarine or butter (Peggy uses margarine)
> **1** large egg
> **⅓** cup milk

Heat oven to 400° F. Put flour, cream of tartar, baking soda, and salt into a large bowl; stir to mix well.

Add margarine and cut in with a pastry blender or rub in with your fingers, until the mixture looks like fine granules.

Beat egg with milk and add to bowl; stir with a fork until a stiff dough forms.

Turn out dough onto a lightly floured surface and give 10 to 15 kneads. Cut dough in half. Knead one half into a ball, turn smooth side up, and pat into a 6-inch circle. Cut into 6 wedges and place apart on an ungreased cookie sheet. Shape remaining dough the same way.

Bake 15 minutes. Remove from oven; turn heat to 200° F. and leave oven door open for 5 minutes. Pull biscuits apart horizontally (or split with a fork) and put halves split side up on the cookie sheet.

Return to oven, close door, and let rusks dry out 1 hour and 15 minutes to 1 hour and 50 minutes, until they are an even, pale brown and crisp and hard throughout. Cool before serving. Store airtight.

NOTE: You can replace the cream of tartar and baking soda with 1 tablespoon baking powder or you can use self-rising flour.

To make round rusks, pat dough to a ¾-inch thickness and cut out 2-inch circles. Makes about 8 biscuits, 16 rusks (including scraps).

TOMATO–SOUR CREAM TART

12 SERVINGS

S erve warm or cold. The tomato is not cooked, but bathed in a rich sour cream dressing. Both the filling and the olive oil biscuit crust can be prepared well ahead of serving.

BISCUIT CRUST

- 1 *cup all-purpose flour*
- 1½ *teaspoons baking powder*
- ½ *teaspoon salt*
- ¼ *cup olive oil*
- ¼ *cup milk*

FILLING

- 2 *large, firm, ripe tomatoes (about 8 ounces each)*
- ¾ *cup sour cream*
- 3 *tablespoons drained, canned, chopped green chilies*
- 2 *teaspoons all-purpose flour*
- ¾ *teaspoon granulated sugar*
- ½ *teaspoon salt*

  Freshly ground pepper, to taste
- 3 *tablespoons thinly sliced green onions (scallions), white and part of the green*

  Thyme and/or parsley sprigs for decoration

Heat oven to 425° F. Put a 10-inch, fluted tart pan with a removable bottom on a cookie sheet.

To make the crust, mix flour, baking powder, and salt in a medium-size bowl. Add olive oil and milk. Stir with a spoon to make a soft, pasty dough.

Put dough between two 12-inch lengths of wax paper and roll into a 12-inch circle. Peel off the top layer of paper. Hold the bottom piece close to the tart pan and flip dough over into the pan. Peel off the wax paper. Fit dough into the pan, pressing it lightly against the sides and patching any tears. Roll the rolling pin across top of pan to remove any excess dough. Bake the crust 11 to 15 minutes, or until evenly browned. Let cool. Remove pan sides.

Meanwhile, organize the filling. Peel tomatoes (dip in boiling water for 15 seconds, then in cold; pull off skins), quarter, and scoop out the seeds. Discard seeds. Cut tomatoes into ¼-inch pieces; you should have about 2 cups. Cover and refrigerate.

In a bowl, mix sour cream, chilies, flour, sugar, salt, and pepper. Add green onions if the tart will be served within a couple of hours. Cover and refrigerate.

Just before serving, drain tomatoes and fold them and the green onions into the sour cream mixture.

To serve cold, slide baked tart shell onto a serving board or plate and spread with tomato filling.

To serve warm, turn the metal rim of the tart pan upside down and rest it loosely on the rim of the crust to prevent it from scorching. Spread tomato filling on the crust. Broil 4 to 5 minutes, just until the filling is warm. Remove pan rim and slide the tart onto a serving board or plate.

Decorate tart with fresh herb sprigs. Cut into wedges.

SAGE BISCUIT WAFERS

Crisp and paper-thin, these are delicious with a glass of wine. For a more substantial snack, serve with Tuna Tapenade (page 101) and crisp celery or radishes.

- *2 cups all-purpose flour*
- *1 tablespoon baking powder*
- *1 teaspoon salt*
- *1 tablespoon dried sage leaves, crumbled, or 2 teaspoons finely chopped fresh sage*
- *½ cup milk*
- *⅓ cup virgin or extra-virgin olive oil*
- *Olive oil and coarse salt, regular salt, or garlic powder*

Heat oven to 425° F. Put flour, baking powder, salt, and sage into a large bowl; stir to mix well. Add milk and olive oil. Stir with a fork until flour mixture is moistened. Gather up with your hands and press into a ball.

Put dough on a lightly floured board and give 10 to 15 kneads. Flatten slightly; cut into 8 wedges. Each wedge will become a wafer. Form one wedge at a time into a ball, and then roll it out on a lightly floured board into a wafer-thin, rough circle 7 to 8 inches in diameter. Brush lightly with olive oil and sprinkle lightly with salt or garlic powder.

Transfer to an ungreased cookie sheet. Bake about 8 minutes, or until light brown. Cool, uncovered, on a wire rack. Serve hot, warm, or cold. Best eaten within 8 hours.

Transfer to an ungreased cookie sheet. Bake about 8 minutes, or until light brown. Cool, uncovered, on a wire rack. Serve hot, warm, or cold. Best eaten within 8 hours.

....

VARIATION

Sage and Sun-Dried Tomato Wafers. After brushing with oil and sprinkling with salt (don't use garlic powder here), wet the undersides of fresh sage leaves or strips of oil-packed sun-dried tomatoes (or both) and arrange them decoratively on top of each circle (4 or 5 leaves to a circle). Cover with a piece of wax paper and roll briefly with rolling pin to affix leaves. Remove wax paper and bake as above.

TAPENADE-TOPPED
MINIATURE BISCUITS

....

60 HORS D'OEUVRES

These olive oil biscuits taste good with almost any flavorful spread. You may freeze the cut-out dough or the baked biscuits.

2 cups all-purpose flour

1 tablespoon baking powder

½ teaspoon salt

½ cup milk

⅓ cup virgin or extra-virgin olive oil

Tuna Tapenade (recipe follows)

Black olive wedges, snipped chives, or tiny sprigs of fresh thyme for garnish

Heat oven to 425° F. Put flour, baking powder, and salt into a large bowl; stir to mix well. Add milk and olive oil. Stir with a fork until the flour mixture is thoroughly moistened. Gather up with your hands and press into a ball.

Put dough on a lightly floured board and give 10 to 15 kneads. Roll out into a ¼-inch-thick round. Cut out with a plain or fluted 1½-inch round biscuit cutter. Place biscuits close together, but not touching, on ungreased cookie sheets.

Bake about 8 minutes, or until pale brown. Slide onto wire racks to cool. If not using within a few hours, store cooled biscuits airtight so they don't dry out.

Not more than 2 hours before serving, top each biscuit with about ½ teaspoon of Tuna Tapenade. Garnish with black olives, chives, or sprigs of thyme.

NOTE: You can use other shaped cutters. There's enough dough to make about 32 2-inch hearts, about 40 2-inch stars.

TUNA TAPENADE

¼ cup olive oil
1 can (2 ounces) anchovy fillets, drained
2 teaspoons drained capers (optional)
1 can (6½ ounces) water- or olive oil-packed tuna, undrained
1 can (about 6 ounces) pitted jumbo ripe olives, drained (about 1⅓ cups)

To make in a food processor, put all ingredients in the work bowl. Process until smooth, about 1 minute.

To make in a blender, pour oil into the container. Add anchovies, capers, and about half of the tuna and olives. Cover and puree to a smooth paste. With machine still running, gradually add remaining olives and tuna, stopping machine three or four times and scraping down sides. Makes about 1¾ cups. Keeps several days in the refrigerator.

CAVIAR STARS

72 2-INCH STARS

Thin, star-shaped biscuits topped with caviar and Crème Fraîche, these are perfect for a holiday party. You can either make the hors d'oeuvres, or simply put out a basket of biscuits alongside bowls of caviar and Crème Fraîche or sour cream (double the amounts) and let the guests top their own. Be sure to roll the dough no thicker than ⅛ inch or the stars will lose their shape during baking.

2 cups all-purpose flour

1 tablespoon baking powder

½ teaspoon salt

5 tablespoons cold unsalted butter, cut up

⅔ cup milk

¼ cup Crème Fraîche (purchased or use recipe page 19) or sour cream

1 to 2 ounces red salmon or other caviar (see note)

2 tablespoons snipped fresh chives or finely chopped sweet onion

Heat oven to 425° F. Put flour, baking powder, and salt into a large bowl; stir to mix well.

Add butter and cut in with a pastry blender or rub in with your fingers, until the mixture looks like fine granules. Add milk and stir with a fork until a soft dough forms. Form dough into a ball, turn out onto a lightly floured surface, and give 10 to 12 kneads.

Roll out dough to an ⅛-inch thickness. Cut out with a 2-inch star cutter. Put on ungreased cookie sheets. Bake 8 to 10 minutes, or until pale brown. Slide onto a wire rack to cool. If not using within an hour or two, store cooled biscuits airtight so they do not dry out.

Up to one hour before serving, top each star with about ¼ teaspoon Crème Fraîche or sour cream and some of the caviar. Sprinkle with chives.

N O T E: This amount of dough also makes about 60 1½-inch round or 32 2-inch heart-shaped biscuits.

Inexpensive caviar with black color added tastes fine on the stars but tends to discolor the cream after standing more than an hour.

INDEX

almond
  -grape shortcake, 58–59
  -orange scones, 82–83
apple lemon-rosemary
    pandowdy, 64–65
apricot swirl scones, 72–73

baking powder biscuits,
    good-with-anything,
    16–17
banana-caramel shortcakes,
    sinfully delicious, 56
barley
  biscuits, 17
  -currant scone, big, 28–29
  drop scones, sweet, 80–81
berry shortcakes, Charlotte
    Walker's, 18–19
biscuit pissaladière, 36–37
blackberries
  Charlotte Walker's break-
    fast berry shortcakes,
    18–19
  summer fruit shortcakes,
    57
blueberry(-ies)
  Charlotte Walker's break-
    fast berry shortcakes,
    18–19
  cobbler, best, 51
  -grape slump, 52–53

summer fruit shortcakes,
    57
buttermilk biscuits, 17

caramel-banana shortcakes,
    sinfully delicious, 56
cardamom-prune drop
    scones, 20–21
caviar stars, 102–103
cheese
  and fresh herb appetizer
    biscuits, 90–91
  scones, Peggy's, 42–43
chocolate-chip scones from
    Plums, 68–69
cinnamon
  biscuit crisps, 78–79
  -pecan rolls, quick, 22–23
cobbler, best blueberry, 51
coffee-hazelnut scones,
    70–71
corn
  biscuit dumplings, ham
    and turnip greens soup
    with, 38–39
  -maple drop biscuits, 15
corn-meal biscuits, 17
cranberry scones, 32–33
crème fraîche, 19
currant
  -barley scone, big, 28–29
  scones, Welsh, 74–75

dumplings, corn biscuit, ham and turnip greens soup with, 38–39

fruit
dried, biscuit strudel, 61–63
summer, shortcakes, 57

gingerbread scones, 67
grape
-almond shortcake, 58–59
-blueberry slump, 52–53

ham
or smoked turkey biscuits, 35
and turnip greens soup with corn biscuit dumplings, 38–39
hamantaschen, 84–85
hazelnut-coffee scones, 70–71
herb, fresh
and cheese appetizer biscuits, 90–91
–olive oil scones, 48–49
hot cross scones, 30–31

lamb potpie Provençale, 40–41
lavender scones, 77

lemon
-rosemary apple pandowdy, 64–65
scones, 77

maple-corn drop biscuits, 15
mushroom appetizer pie, fresh, 92–93

oat
biscuits, 17
drop scones, sweet, 81
onion(s)
biscuit pissaladière, 36–37
-potato flat pie, 44–45
orange-almond scones, 82–83

pecan-cinnamon rolls, quick, 22–23
pie
Canadian pork, 46–47
fresh mushroom appetizer, 92–93
lamb pot-, Provençale, 40–41
potato-onion flat, 44–45
pork pie, Canadian, 46–47
potato(es)
Mother Bathia's Scottish tattie scones, 26–27
-onion flat pie, 44–45
potpie, lamb Provençale, 40–41

preserves, refrigerator straw-
    berry, 87
pretzels, black pepper
    biscuit, 89
prune-cardamom drop
    scones, 20–21

raisin(s)
    dried fruit biscuit strudel,
        61–63
    scones, 24–25
rosemary-lemon apple
    pandowdy, 64–65
rusks, Peggy Primrose
    Alston's Suffolk, 94–95
rye biscuits, 17

sage biscuit wafers, 98–99
samosa flat pie, 45
scented geranium scones, 77
shortcake(s)
    almond-grape, 58–59
    Charlotte Walker's break-
        fast berry, 18–19
    Ellen Lansing's strawberry,
        54–55
    sinfully delicious caramel-
        banana, 56
    summer fruit, 57
    tips, 60
slump, blueberry-grape,
    52–53

soup, ham and turnip greens,
    with corn biscuit dump-
    lings, 38–39
sour cream–tomato tart,
    96–97
strawberry(-ies)
    Charlotte Walker's break-
        fast berry shortcakes,
        18–19
    preserves, refrigerator, 87
    shortcakes, Ellen Lans-
        ing's, 54–55
    summer fruit shortcakes,
        57
strudel, dried fruit biscuit,
    61–63

tapenade-topped miniature
    biscuits, 100–101
tart, tomato–sour cream,
    96–97
tea, a Devonshire cream, 86
tomato(es):
    biscuit pissaladière, 36–37
    –sour cream tart, 96–97
    sun-dried, and sage
        wafers, 99
turkey, smoked, or ham
    biscuits, 35

whole-wheat
    –raisin scones, coarse, 25
    scones, sweet, 77